English Grammar and Composition Workbook

A Workbook and Activity Book for Students of Continuing education of CBSE, ICSE and State Boards.

Chandan Sengupta

Creative Learning Series

English Grammar and Composition Workbook

A Workbook and Activity Book for Students of Continuing Education of CBSE, ICSE and State Boards.

Focus: CBSE, ICSE, GCSE, Olympiads, state Boards and School Level Challenges

Chandan Sengupta

This workbook is prepared to address the need of fellow aspirants of different competitive examinations duly conducted time to time by various boards of studies. We also wanted to cover up the need of students having eagerness to develop their skills through self studies. It is not merely a gguide book. This workbook cannot introduce any learner simply to the mechanism of correct use of grammar related rules of speaking and writing. Primary knowledge of Grammar and Composition is required before moving through this workbook.

Types of questions asked in exams are of similar pattern. Contents, in some cases, may differ. These materials are collected from our daily use of English. It would be better if fellow students start talking in English in a group made up of few of the selected friends working in a closed user group. It would be more convenient if such group start interacting through electronic media and through other suitable means. Another fruitful initiative will be following electronic media, news channels, analytics and other sources of information and views so as to collections of vocabulary will be increased. Collection and use of new words will definitely increase the grasping of students on the process of writing and representation of facts in speech. One can even aspire for an enhancement in the linguistic skill by following stories and compositions made by famous authors. Initiatives of any kind will be accepted and quantified in accord to the coverage of selected areas of competencies. The related fields of studies are linked together in such a way that they cannot be addressed individually through focused study materials. We simply put them in a definite order to link up our efforts to gain linguistic competencies of desired types..

This Book is prepared for fellow aspirants of Continuing Education.

Contents

Points to Remember

1. The compound personal pronouns may be used as the objects of transitive verbs or of prepositions when the object denotes the same person or thing as the subject.
2. In this use they are called reflexive pronouns.
3. King Alfred interested himself in his subjects
4. Some words are used either as adjectives or as pronouns. Such words are called adjective pronouns.
5. The demonstratives are this (plural, these), that (plural, those). They point out persons or things for special attention
6. The indefinite pronouns point out objects less clearly or definitely than demonstratives do.
7. Most indefinites may be either pronouns or adjectives. But none is always a substantive in modern use, and every is always an adjective.
8. Each other and one another are regarded as compound pronouns. They designate related persons or things.
   - My neighbor and I like each other.
9. All, several, few, many, and similar words are often classed as indefinites. They may be used as adjectives or as substantives. Everybody, everything, anybody, anything, somewhat, aught, naught,20 etc., are called indefinite nouns.
10. Relative pronouns have a peculiar function in the sentence, since they serve both as pronouns and as connectives. Their use may be seen by comparing the two sentences that follow:—
    - 1. This is the sailor, and he saved my life.
11. Relative pronouns connect dependent clauses with main clauses by referring directly to a substantive in the main clause
12. The simple relative pronouns are who, which, that, as, and what.
13. Who is either masculine or feminine; which and what are neuter; that and as are of all three genders.
    - All who heard, approved.
14. A relative pronoun must agree with its antecedent in gender, number, and person.
    - It is I who am wrong. [First person, singular number: antecedent, I.]

- The road that leads to the shore is sandy. [Third person singular: antecedent, road.]

15. A relative pronoun in the objective case is often omitted.

16. Certain questions of gender call for particular attention.
1. Which is commonly used in referring to the lower animals unless these are regarded as persons. This is true even when he or she is used of the same animals
17. In the case of things without animal life, of which and whose are both common. The tendency is to prefer of which in prose, but whose is often used because of its more agreeable sound. In poetry, whose is especially frequent.

- Jack was fishing with a bamboo rod, to the end of which he had tied a short piece of ordinary twine.

18. The clause introduced by a relative pronoun is an adjective clause, since it serves as an adjective modifier of the antecedent
19. A relative pronoun that serves merely to introduce a descriptive fact is called a descriptive relative.
20. A relative pronoun that introduces a clause confining or limiting the application of the antecedent is called a restrictive relative.
21. Before a descriptive relative we regularly make a pause in speaking, but never before a restrictive relative.
22. A descriptive relative is preceded by a comma; a restrictive relative is not.

- Three sailors, who were loitering on the pier, sprang to the rescue.

23. The relative pronoun what is equivalent to that which, and has a double construction:—(1) the construction of the omitted or implied antecedent (that); (2) the construction of the relative (which).
24. The compound relative pronouns may include or imply their own antecedents and hence may have a double construction.
25. Whoever calls, he must be admitted. [Here he, the antecedent of whoever, is the subject of must be admitted, and whoever is the subject of calls.]

- He shall have whatever he wishes.

26. The interrogative pronouns are who, which, and what. They are used in asking questions

- Whose voice is that?
- Which shall I take?

- Which is correct?

27. An adjective is said to belong to the substantive which it describes or limits.

28. An adjective which describes is called a descriptive adjective; one which points out or designates is called a definitive adjective

29. A proper noun used as an adjective, or an adjective derived from a proper noun, is called a proper adjective and usually begins with a capital letter.

30. Definitive adjectives include:—pronouns used as adjectives (as, this opportunity; those pictures; either table; what time is it?);

31. Adjectives may be classified, according to their position in the sentence, as attributive, appositive, and predicate adjectives.

32. An attributive adjective is closely attached to its noun and regularly precedes it.

- The angry spot doth glow on Cæsar's brow.

33. A predicate adjective completes the meaning of the predicate verb, but describes or limits the subject.

34. The adjectives a (or an) and the are called articles.

1. The definite article the points out one or more particular objects as distinct from others of the same kind.

35. The indefinite article a (or an) designates an object as merely one of a general class or kind.

- Lend me a pencil.

36. An adjective preceded by the may be used as a plural noun.

- The brave are honored.

37. An is used before words beginning with a vowel or silent h; a before other words. Thus,—

- an owl;

38. The degrees of comparison indicate by their form in what degree of intensity the quality described by the adjective exists.

39. There are three degrees of comparison,—the positive, the comparative, and the superlative.

40. The comparative degree of an adjective is formed by adding the termination er to the positive degree.

41. It denotes that the quality exists in the object described in a higher degree than in some other object.

42. Adjectives ending in silent e drop this letter before the comparative ending er and the superlative ending est. Thus,—

- wise, wiser, wisest;

43. Many adjectives are compared by prefixing the adverbs more and most to the positive degree.
    - recent, more recent, most recent;
44. An adverb is a word which modifies a verb, an adjective, or another adverb.
    - The storm ceased suddenly.
45. Adverbs are classified according to their meaning as: (1) adverbs of manner; (2) adverbs of time; (3) adverbs of place; (4) adverbs of degree
46. There is often used merely to introduce a sentence in the inverted order
    - There are many strangers in town.
47. Relative adverbs introduce subordinate clauses and are similar in their use to relative pronouns.
48. I know a farmhouse {in which | where} we can spend the night.

49. The principal relative adverbs are:—where, whence, whither, wherever, when, whenever, while, as, how, why, before, after, till, until, since.
50. An interrogative adverb introduces a question.
51. Where, when, whence, whither, how, why, may be used as interrogative adverbs.
52. Most adverbs are compared by means of more and most.
    - Richard came more promptly than John. [Comparative.]
    - Henry came most promptly of all. [Superlative.]
53. The comparative degree, not the superlative, is used in comparing two persons or things.
54. When two adjectives or adverbs are contrasted by means of than, more is used with the first.
    - Such indulgence is more kind than wise.
55. Words indicating number are called numerals. They are adjectives, nouns, or adverbs.
    - There are seven days in the week. [Adjective.]
56. Cardinal numeral adjectives (one, two, three, four, etc.) are used in counting, and answer the question "How many?"
57. Ordinal numeral adjectives (first, second, third, etc.) denote the position or order of a person or thing in a series.
    - Carl plays the second violin.
58. All the cardinal and ordinal numerals may become nouns and may take a plural ending in some of their senses.
    - One is enough.
    - The nine played an excellent game.

- Three twos are six.

59. Certain numeral adjectives (single, double, triple, etc.) indicate how many times a thing is taken or of how many like parts it consists.

    - A double row of policemen stood on guard.

60. Certain numeral adverbs and adverbial phrases indicate how many times an action takes place.

    - Once my assailant slipped.

61. A verb is a word which can assert something (usually an action) concerning a person, place, or thing

    - 1.We jumped for joy.
    - Rabbits burrow into the sides of hills.

62. Certain verbs, when used to make verb-phrases, are called auxiliary (that is, "aiding") verbs, because they help other verbs to express action or state of some particular kind

63. Verbs are either transitive or intransitive

64. Some verbs may be followed by a substantive denoting that which receives the action or is produced by it. These are called transitive verbs. All other verbs are called intransitive.

65. A verb which is transitive in one of its senses may be intransitive in another.

66. Many transitive verbs may be used absolutely,—that is, merely to express action without any indication of the direct object.

67. Is (in its various forms) and several other verbs may be used to frame sentences in which some word or words in the predicate describe or define the subject

68. A participle is said to belong to the substantive which it describes or limits.

    - Rising, she opened the window. [Rising belongs to she.]
    - I heard the rain falling. [Falling belongs to the object rain.]

69. A participle should not be used without some substantive to which it may belong.

    - RIGHT: Entering the room, we saw a strange sight. [The participle entering belongs to the pronoun we.]

70. A participle may take an object if its meaning allows.

    - Lifting the box, he moved toward the door.

71. The past participle is often used as a predicate adjective expressing state or condition.

    - When the rain at last ceased, we were drenched [that is, very wet].

72. A substantive, with the participle belonging to it, is often used to make a peculiar form of adverbial modifying phrase The wind failing, we lowered the sail.

73. A substantive, with a participle, may express the cause, time, or circumstances of an action. This is called the absolute construction.

74. The substantive is in the nominative case and is called a nominative absolute.

- Two days having elapsed, we again set forward. [The phrase in italics is equivalent to when two days had elapsed: it expresses time.]
- This done, proceed to business. [The phrase this done is equivalent to the clause since (or when) this is done, and indicates cause or time.]

75. From nearly every English verb there may be formed a verbal noun in -ing.

76. Verbal nouns in -ing have the form of present participles, but the construction of nouns.

77. They are often called participial nouns.

78. Verbal nouns in -ing may take a direct or an indirect object if their meaning allows.

- Digging gold seems to the uninitiated like finding buried treasure.

79. A verbal noun in -ing may take an adverbial modifier.

80. But verbal nouns in -ing, like other nouns, may be modified by adjectives.

- Extemporaneous speaking is good practice.

81. To the verbal nouns being and having, past participles may be attached, so as to give the effect of voice and tense.

- There were grave doubts expressed as to his having seen the mastodon.
- After having been treated in so harsh a fashion, I had no wish to repeat the interview.

82. Verbal nouns in -ing are similar in some of their constructions to infinitives used as nouns

Preface

Examination is a process through which some of the candidates from a large population are to be selected for fulfilling a particular purpose. Students in general are job seekers, but few of them learn for gaining personal enhancement. They also move on in search of some study materials which can equip them positively so that a considerable ace can be obtained while addressing questions of specific types in examination.

Expectation of parents from their ward resides primarily on the aspect of a gain of high score in examination. They also imply their burden of expectations on the fellow student without considering the level of emotions and bands of feelings. Choice factor, wills and wishes of fellow students should be addressed a little so as to ensure their effective participation in the process of examination and evaluation. Fear of examination is generally developed due to the kinds of expectations their parents and other associates imposed upon the ward. It also takes a shape of fear due to the pre-determined idea of the development of agony in the condition if examination results go down. Exam fear itself eats u a considerable part of memory by diverting waves of thinking towards gaining a preparedness which is required to face some sort of adverse situation during the down play duly anticipated by the ward in advance.

How to overcome?

Matter is very simple as well as easy to follow.

1.   Prepare a time bound task and maintain the same throughout the academic session.

2.   Take support of some standard books on the basis of the types of inputs you want.

3.   Consider examination as a part of life as we have to appear periodically all the time up to a prolonged span of our life.

4.   Examination also provides us a scope of assessing our own levels of understanding and we should move on through rectification process instead of crying for the performance or score of desired levels duly expected by elders.

5.   Examination cannot be considered as any mode of status with which we are to exhibit some superiority on others. It should not be taken as a status symbol or a scale of gradation in society.

6.   Examination is not the ultimate state of scaling through which we judge the performance of a student in real life situation.

7.   There are lots of other sectors of life for which there is no examination: how pa person is talking; how a person is using words while making some good sentences; the capability of a person to establish and maintain relationship with others; effort of performing a task whenever chance comes; healing others if asked for etc. are some of the hundreds of scaling through which a personality can be judged.

8.   Our school system cannot consider all the parameters of scaling to say the level of the personality of a student.

9.   There are thousands of cross-academic as well as hybrid faculties available to be opted by students in society. That is why dying for only selected faculty and hunting for money cannot be considered as any brilliant idea.

10.   One should have positive mental attitude towards addressing issues and concerns in daily life.

11.   Regular study is most important and effective too than compared to intensive study of a short period of time.

12.   We always rely upon other non-standard process due to their cheap availability. One should not compromise with quality.

13.   Treasure of knowledge never moves towards us, but we have to move towards the treasure of knowledge.

14.   There are several sources available in market from which the basic modules required for a specific purpose to be fulfilled can be obtained and also can be worked out for accelerating the regularised study.

Volume of practice material is less important than the strategy with which such volume of practice materials can be used or re-arranged.

There are millions of books available in market which can introduce a learner to English language and English grammar. More discussed theme of language learning is the English Grammar. This effort came in focus due to the increasing demand of people from different walks of life regarding the type of workbook which can equip a student in a specific way in terms of the enhancement of language related skills.

This workbook is designed to provide additional study materials to fellow students of High School standards. They equip themselves differently by making them fit for forthcoming examination. Learning by doing is the best way of acquiring such kinds of skills in stipulated time frame.

A language stands upon its rules of grammar and compositions. Similar mechanism is applicable to English also. It has such kinds of sets of rules through which one can aspire for the attainment of a perfectness in writing and expressions.

English as a language is not so difficult for any non-English person. The basic structure of English language is user friendly and is also of a comprehensive type. Modern instruments are also much friendly with this language. Because of this reason and some other, English as a user friendly language is becoming popular day by day. Number of people from non-English community who can read, write and speak English quite fluently are growing in number day by day. They are also taking different roles assigned to them in the cosmopolitan environment.

Non-English learners and aspirants often feel difficulties in pronunciation English words properly with needful tunings. These difficulties often become a serious obstacle while some English people go on trying to establish communication with them. Due to such difficulties also they often become disqualified in proving their capabilities of doing something fruitful.

This workbook and practice manual will provide an ample scope of gaining adequate skill and competence in linguistic communication. Stress is implied in the portions related to grammar and composition of the language so as to enhance the related skills and competences of the fellow learner.

It is also recommended that one should go on practicing related exercises alongside the referral readings for the purpose of gaining proficiency. A discussion on the common mistakes related to the grammar and composition of this language is also included for the purpose of drawing attention of fellow students and aspirants towards the content areas of the communication techniques.

English as a language came to India along with the colonial rule. They people felt it necessary to educate a considerable part of Indian as well as Asian communities in English for ensuring their service lines in the colonies. It was more perfectly pitched in through religious propagations.

People of India accepted the language gladly and started getting adjusted with the cultural bands of English orientation. This West Germanic language is developed from Anglo-Frician dialects. This dialect is brought to Britain during 6th to 7th Century by Anglo-Saxon Migrants. In due course of time this language developed considerably and transformed into the dialect of modern time. Anglo –Saxon dialect was more commonly known as old-English. Near about 400 Latin loan Words were introduced in English alongside the advent of Christianity. During the development Middle English near about 10,000 loan words from French origin entered the English dialect and made it an enriched one. Fully developed English dictionary, the Dictionary of the English Language, was published by Samuel Johnson in 1755. English Grammar by Pristle was an added contribution in the line of development of English Language. In modern time the total English speaking community worldwide may exceed 1.5 billion mark! There are several other instances to ascertain the fact regarding the ever increasing popularity of the International Language. It has also secured a prominent position in the international arena as a common dialect that people can opt with an ease.

After becoming assured about the ever increasing popularity of this language we can now imply adequate focus on the development of skills and competence of our fellow students and aspirants through exposing them to the horizon of interactive parts related to perfect and advanced English dialect. We also expect a timely participation of fellow scholars in this effort. They can continue evaluating their own skills through learning continuity supplemented with self paced evaluations.

Evolution of English Pronoun is another additional advantage of the modern English. Conflated forms of pronouns are also called an objective case. Development of such name is only because it is used only for objects of verbs. Once in old English there was distinct case system for both accusative and dative purposes. Later on such system collapsed into a single system of object (oblique) case having utility for objects of either a verb or a preposition. Studies in English were introduced in different universities during 19th and 20th Century because of its continuous developments in non-European continents. Development of such study was remarkably high in USA during 1970s. It was also due to incorporation of English as another official language in most of the countries in the world.

Different courses in English are meant for different purposes. Studies in English are further accelerated with the advent of Informatics and allied fields. We consider English as a second language (a language study meant for non-English person). Errors in English are mainly observed from the field of syntax error, vocabulary error and error related to punctuations. Rules in English are periodically introduced by different scholars time to time. Not to terminate a sentence by preposition, for an example, was the another rule introduced by Robert Lowth .

Chandan Sukumar Sengupta

How to Speak!

Will you speak properly when chances come?

It is really a difficult question. There are different types of individuals: some prefer speaking properly to explain things in a better way, some other person prefer writing in a structured way rather than speaking in public. English Grammar provides basic template for both types of aspirants and continuously providing aids for fulfilling the same purpose. Some individuals never prefer speaking even though they maintain a considerable volume of vocabulary. There are individuals who can speak fluently by using their limited collection of vocabulary. Fluency in speaking can be gained only after establishment of adequate command over vocabulary. We also facilitate the fellow learner in different possible way to gain such mastery. Passages from interesting events and popular scriptures can be used for comprehension and guided practice for increasing the duration of study of a student.

Here also we are trying to move through the same strategy by making students involved in different kinds of background study material collected periodically from different sources.

Speaking is obviously a kind of activity which requires collection and maintenance of an extended format of words and their collocations in a definite fashion to cultivate an idea of using best possible combination of words while speaking. It may be in the form of a word tree, a network of words, a collocation table or some other creative alternatives which is convenient and easy to access.

Word class table can give us a better understanding of particular category of words to be considered while speaking or writing a broad spectrum composition. We can also correlate words in framing different types of sentences on the basis of linked and correlated words. An example of such kind of linked words is advanced for providing a basic understanding of the concept.

Revision Works

1. Using the Past Continuous tense, fill in the blanks with the correct forms of the verbs shown in brackets. For example:

    I ___________ a salad. (to make)

    I was making a salad.

    They ___________ to find some boots. (to try)

    They were trying to find some boots.

1. He _______________ a book. (to read)

2. We _________________ money. (to save)

3. She _______________ school. (to attend)

4. It _________________. (to thunder)

5. They ________________ for the exam. (to study)

6. We ________________ ourselves. (to sun)

7. They _______________ they way. (to lead)

8. You ______________ by bus. (to leave)

9. We ________________ through the snow. (to plod)

10. You _______________ your goals. (to attain)

2. Rewrite the following affirmative statements as questions, negative statements, negative questions without contractions, negative questions with contractions, and affirmative statements followed by negative tag questions. For example:

    You were learning French.   Were you learning French?

    You were not learning French.   Were you not learning French?

    Weren't you learning French?

You were learning French, weren't you?

1. We were starting a business.   2. She was waiting outside.

3. He was singing.

3. Using the Past Continuous tense, fill in the blanks with the correct forms of the verbs shown in brackets. For example:

_____ you _______ last night? (to work)

Were you working last night?

It ___ not _______. (to rain)   It was not raining.

They _____________ home. (to hurry) They were hurrying home.

1. We ________________ for the test. (to prepare)

2. _______ she __________ notes? (to take)

3. I _______ not __________ long. (to wait)

4. They ________________ at Woolco. (to shop)

5. _______ it not __________ outside? (to freeze)

6. She ________________ on Almond Street last year. (to live)

7. _______ you ___________ supper when the phone rang? (to eat)

8. He ________________ asleep by the time the lesson ended. (to fall)

9. _______ we not ___________ the next chapter? (to discuss)

10. They ___________ their books away, when their friends arrived. (to put)

11. You _______ not ____________ the news. (to follow)

12. _______ I ____________ too much noise? (to make)

4. Using the Past Perfect tense, fill in the blanks with the correct forms of the verbs shown in brackets. For example:

I _________ the parcel. (to open)   I had opened the parcel.

They ________ to the opera. (to be) They had been to the opera.

1. She ________________ a sweater. (to buy)

2. He ________________ to work. (to start)

3. You ________________ the message. (to understand)

4. We ________________ the appointment. (to forget)

5. They ________________ us. (to convince)

6. She ________________ the book. (to find)

7. He ________________ the envelope. (to tear)

8. You ________________ your breakfast. (to finish)

9. We _______________ to school. (to go)

10. They ________________ the beds. (to make)

5. Rewrite the following affirmative statements as questions, negative statements, negative questions without contractions, negative questions

with contractions, and affirmative statements followed by negative tag questions. For example:

He had attended the concert.   Had he attended the concert?

He had not attended the concert. Had he not attended the concert?

    Hadn't he attended the concert?

    He had attended the concert, hadn't he?

1. You had entered the contest.   2. I had wanted to come.

3. We had arrived on time.

6. Using the Past Perfect tense, fill in the blanks with the correct forms of the verbs shown in brackets. For example:

    He _____________ hard. (to practise)   He had practised hard.

    ___ they _____ a good job? (to do)   Had they done a good job?

    I ___ not _____ the news. (to hear)

    I had not heard the news.

1. You _________________ it carefully.(to consider)

2. She _________________ her way in the woods. (to lose)

3. _____ he not ____________ his hands? (to wash)

4. _____ they ___________ the letter? (to read)

5. I _____ not _____________ the words. (to forget)

6. We ___________ to come even before we received the letter. (to decide)

7. _____ he not ____________ everything well? (to organize)

8. They _____ not __________ a holiday in a long time. (to have)

9. She ________________ to talk to us. (to stop)

10. He _____ not yet ____________. (to arrive)

11. _____ you __________ to meet him? (to plan)

12. I _____ not ___________ her for a long time. (to see)

7. Using the Past Perfect Continuous tense, fill in the blanks with the correct forms of the verbs shown in brackets. For example:

    We _________________ for an apartment. (to search)

    We had been searching for an apartment.

    She _______________ extra courses. (to take)

She had been taking extra courses.

1. We ___________________ the grass. (to cut)

2. You ___________________ at the photographs. (to look)

3. They ___________________ you the letters. (to give)

4. He ___________________ for us. (to wait)

5. She ___________________ a business. (to run)

6. It ___________________ all night. (to rain)

7. We ___________________ them. (to encourage)

8. You ___________________ on the beach. (to lie)

9. They ___________________ the sauce. (to taste)

10. He ___________________ behind. (to lag)

8. Rewrite the following affirmative statements as questions, negative statements, negative questions without contractions, negative questions with contractions, and affirmative statements followed by negative tag questions. For example:

She had been keeping a diary.   Had she been keeping a diary?

She had not been keeping a diary. Had she not been keeping a diary?

Hadn't she been keeping a diary?

She had been keeping a diary, hadn't she?

1. We had been raking the leaves.

2. You had been visiting your cousins.

3. They had been swimming in the lake.

9. Using the Past Perfect Continuous tense, fill in the blanks with the correct forms of the verbs shown in brackets. For example:

We ___________. (to argue)   We had been arguing.

___ he ___________ well? (to feel)   Had he been feeling well?

I ___ not ___________ much walking. (to do)

I had not been doing much walking.

1. You ___________________ the stove. (to clean)

2. She _______ not ___________________ regularly. (to come)

3. _______ they not ___________________ on you? (to count)

4. We ___________________ for shoes. (to look)

5. _______ it not ___________________ that day? (to snow)

6. I ___________________ for groceries. (to shop)

7. _____ he not _____________________ to the news? (to listen)

8. They _____ not _____________________ to drive far. (to intend)

9. _____ we _____________________ on time? (to leave)

10. _____ you _____________________ that? (to expect)

11. They _____________________ television. (to watch)

12. He _____ not _____________________ long when the bus arrived. (to wait)

10. For each of the following sentences, paying attention to whether the underlined auxiliary is a form of to be, to do or to have, fill in the blank with the bare infinitive, present participle, or past participle of the verb given in brackets, as appropriate. Refer if necessary to the table summarizing the formation of the English present and past tenses. For example:

He was _________ medicine. (to study)

He was studying medicine.

You have _______ the food. (to bring)

You have brought the food.

We had been _______ a long time. (to wait)

We had been waiting a long time.

Does she _______ classical music? (to like)

Does she like classical music?

1. She was _____________________ a picture. (to draw)

2. We have _____________________ our homework. (to finish)

3. I have been _____________________ for an opportunity. (to wait)

4. Do you _____________________ a bicycle? (to own)

5. We are _____________________ coffee. (to drink)

6. Did he _____________________ the book? (to enjoy)

7. They were _____________________ us. (to expect)

8. You had _____________________ a job. (to find)

9. He is _____________________ the truth. (to tell)

10. It had been _____________________ all morning. (to snow)

11. We had _____________________ the window. (to open)

12. I am _____________________ potatoes. (to peel)

13. You did not _____________________ my letter. (to answer)

14. It does not _____________________. (to matter)

15. I have _____________________ this movie before. (to see)

11. Make the following statements emphatic. For example:

He likes cats.	He does like cats.
You have finished.	You have finished.
They were here.	They were here.
We are not ready.	We are not ready.

1. I enjoy reading.	2. They do not like music.
3. It snowed.	4. I have found my pen.
5. She cooks well.	6. You were listening to the radio.
7. They found the answer.	8. He was right.
9. She understands.	10. They had locked the door.
11. He did not arrive late.	12. You ran fast.

Answers

1. was reading 2. were saving 3. was attending 4. was thundering 5. were studying 6. were sunning 7. were leading 8. were leaving 9. were plodding 10. were attaining

to Exercise 2:

1. Were we starting a business? We were not starting a business. Were we not starting a business? Weren't we starting a business? We were starting a business, weren't we?

2. Was she waiting outside? She was not waiting outside. Was she not waiting outside? Wasn't she waiting outside? She was waiting outside, wasn't she?

3. Was he singing? He was not singing. Was he not singing? Wasn't he singing? He was singing, wasn't he?

to Exercise 3:

1. were preparing 2. Was, taking 3. was, waiting 4. were shopping 5. Was, freezing 6. was living 7. Were, eating 8. was falling 9. Were, discussing 10. were putting 11. were, following 12. Was, making

to Exercise 4:

1. had bought 2. had started 3. had understood 4. had forgotten 5. had convinced 6. had found 7. had torn 8. had finished 9. had gone 10. had made

to Exercise 5:

1. Had you entered the contest? You had not entered the contest. Had you not entered the contest? Hadn't you entered the contest? You had entered the contest, hadn't you?

2. Had I wanted to come? I had not wanted to come. Had I not wanted to come? Hadn't I wanted to come? I had wanted to come, hadn't I?

3. Had we arrived on time? We had not arrived on time. Had we not arrived on time? Hadn't we arrived on time? We had arrived on time, hadn't we?

to Exercise 6:

1. had considered 2. had lost 3. Had, washed 4. Had, read 5. had, forgotten 6. had decided 7. Had, organized 8. had, had 9. had stopped 10. had, arrived 11. Had, planned 12. had, seen

to Exercise 7:

1. had been cutting 2. had been looking 3. had been giving 4. had been waiting 5. had been running 6. had been raining 7. had been encouraging 8. had been lying 9. had been tasting 10. had been lagging

to Exercise 8:

1. Had we been raking the leaves? We had not been raking the leaves. Had we not been raking the leaves? Hadn't we been raking the leaves? We had been raking the leaves, hadn't we?

2. Had you been visiting your cousins? You had not been visiting your cousins. Had you not been visiting your cousins? Hadn't you been visiting your cousins? You had been visiting your cousins, hadn't you?

3. Had they been swimming in the lake? They had not been swimming in the lake. Had they not been swimming in the lake? Hadn't they been swimming in the lake? They had been swimming in the lake, hadn't they?

to Exercise 9:

1. had been cleaning 2. had/been coming 3. Had/been counting 4. had been looking 5. Had/been snowing 6. had been shopping 7. Had/ been listening 8. had/been intending 9. Had/been leaving 10. Had/ been expecting 11. had been watching 12. had/been waiting

to Exercise 10:
1. drawing 2. finished 3. waiting 4. own 5. drinking 6. enjoy 7. expecting 8. found 9. telling 10. snowing 11. opened 12. peeling 13. answer 14. matter 15. seen

to Exercise 11: 1. I do enjoy reading. 2. They do not like music. 3. It did snow. 4. I have found my pen. 5. She does cook well. 6. You were listening to the radio. 7. They did find the answer. 8. He was right. 9. She does understand. 10. They had locked the door. 11. He did not arrive late. 12. You did run fast.

***

.

2. Test Paper I

Language is an important part of communication. It also displays quality of a person at different instances.

- Chandan Sengupta

01. Sit …, please!
a) down   b) about
02. Come …! Hurry up!
a) after
b) on
c) backwards
03. Today we need to weigh … all the pros and cons.
a) after
b) up
c) on
04. The student continued learning … of the noise.
a) despite
b) although
c) in spite
05. She washed her car.
a) itself
b) herself
c) on his own
06. A new villa can … .
a) be built

b) built
c) building
07. They mustn't … .

c) within
a) punishing
b) be punished
c) had been punished
08. Might they … by me?
a) be invited
b) invite
c) inviting
09. She is to … here at four.
a) arriving
b) arrived
c) arrive
10. No sooner … at the station than the night train left.
a) had I arrive
b) had I arrived
c) arrived had I
11. While they were having a break, we … negotiations.
a) had been having
b) were having
c) have been having
12. Where … your sister been?
a) was
b) has

c) will
13. Choose the correct sentence:
a) We have never been friends. We have almost nothing in common.
b) We never were friends. We have almost nothing in common.
c) We had never been friend. We have almost nothing in common.
14. His wife has … him and everything is fine between them.
a) forgived
b) forgotten
c) forgiven

15. They have … me. I will explain it again.
a) misunderstood
b) misunderstand
c) misunderstanding
16. She … the book because she had enjoyed it a long time ago.
a) reread
b) reading
c) had reread
17. I … the heating system since last Monday.
a) haven't checked
b) haven't checking
c) didn't check
18. How long … the institution?
a) have they be controlling
b) have they been controlling
c) had they been controlled
19. He said he … for two hours.

a) was working
b) has been working
c) had been working
2020. I read they … the assassin.
a) punish
b) be punished
c) had punished
2021. Choose the correct sentence:
a) It has already been said.
b) It was already said.
c) It will already be said.
22. If I were you, I … choose another team member.
a) will
b) would
c) would have chosen
23. I … improve my German as soon as possible.
a) must

b) must have
c) must be
24. This capital is crowded … tourists.
a) of
b) about
c) with
25. The new colleague is full … innovative ideas.
a) in
b) about
c) of
26. I'm fed up … this job.
a) with
b) about

c) of

27. I was impressed … her beauty.
a) of
b) by
c) about

28. I'm really serious … everything.
a) at
b) of
c) about

29. I'm so excited … the vaccine news.
a) about
b) in
c) on

30. I don't know why she is so pessimistic … their future.
a) with
b) about
c) of

31. It's very nice … you to remember it.
a) to
b) of
c) with

32. I have just arrived … the airport.
a) in
b) about
c) at

33. What's the difference … these two laptops?
a) between
b) among
c) of

34. See you … two months.
a) of
b) with
c) in

35. Tim said: "I don't teach German.".
a) Tim said that he doesn't teach German.
b) Tim said that he didn't teach German.
c) Tim said that he haven't taught German.

36. The patient said: "I'm experiencing a strange feeling.".
a) The patient said that he was experiencing a strange feeling.
b) The patient said that he has been experiencing a strange feeling.
c) The patient said that he had been experiencing a strange feeling.

37. John said: "She has sung a beautiful song.".
a) John said that she has sung a beautiful song.
b) John said that she was singing a beautiful song.
c) John said that she had sung a beautiful song.

38. We … Russian for an hour by the time she enters the room.
a) are speaking
b) will have been speaking
c) would have been speaking

39. I … English for five years by next year.

a) will have been teaching
b) will teach
c) will be teaching
40. They asked me: "Did they destroy that building?".
a) They asked me they had destroyed that building.

b) They asked me if they had destroyed that building.
c) They asked me if they destroyed that building.
41. The journalist asked me: "Is he accusing her?".
a) The journalist asked me if he had been accusing her.
b) The journalist asked me if he has been accusing her.
c) The journalist asked me if he was accusing her.
42. My wife asked me: "How long have you been dating with her?".
a) My wife asked me how long I'm dating with her.
b) My wife asked me how long I had been dating with her.
c) My wife asked me how long I was dating with her.
43. Choose the correct sentence:
a) Doesn't she like this phone?
b) Not she like this phone?
c) Didn't she liked this phone?
44. Choose the correct sentence:
a) Wasn't it not obvious?
b) Didn't it been obvious?
c) Was it not obvious?

45. Choose the correct sentence:
a) Who are you talking?
b) Who are you talk to?
c) Who are you talking to?
46. Choose the correct sentence:
a) Who is this gift for?
b) Whom does this gift for?
c) Who is this gift?
47. It's the most … song.
a) fame
b) famous
c) famously
48. What do you know about the world of …?
a) fashion
b) fashionable
c) fashioning

49. It was a … experiment regarding new treatments.
a) science
b) sciencely
c) scientific
50. …, what he is saying is true.
a) Actually
b) Recently
c) Actual
51. Turn … the sound! It's way too loud.
a) up
b) away
c) down
52. I switched … the laptop.
a) off
b) about
c) away

53. Sarah showed … at the end of the party.
a) within
b) up
c) beyond
54. Our plan fell … . We'll try again soon.
a) away
b) through
c) about
55. Choose the correct sentence:
a) I'm trying to learn German in spite of not having enough free time.
b) I'm trying to learn German in spite to have enough free time.
c) I'm trying to learn German despite of having enough free time.
56. I … sooner go abroad.
a) had
b) could
c) would
57. There is no point …, so let's calm down.
a) argue

b) in arguing
c) to argue
58. The mission … last week.
a) should be cancelled
b) should have been cancelled
c) should cancel
59. Whatever you say, it … change my life.
a) was
b) has

c) did
60. Not only … but I also work.
a) I study
b) do I study
c) had I study
61. Choose the correct sentence:
a) Do you work next Friday?
b) Are you working next Friday?
c) Have you worked next Friday?
62. Choose the correct sentence:
a) I'm tasting this dish now.
b) I taste the dish now.
c) I've been tasting this dish now.
63. Choose the correct sentence:
a) She's owing me 300 dollars now.
b) She's been owing me 300 dollars now.
c) She owes me 300 dollars now.
64. Is the following sentence correct? "I was wanting to help them."
a) correct
b) incorrect
65. Is the following sentence correct? "Were you knowing all the truth at that moment?"
a) correct
b) incorrect
66. My old family friend … invited me.
a) will

b) should

c) have

67. She … brilliant results.

a) showed

b) shown

c) has showing

68. The manager said he … those employees.

a) hadn't fired

b) doesn't fires

c) will fire

69. When she noticed me I … the car for two hours.

a) was driving

b) had been driving

c) have been driving

70. Necessary conditions … now.

a) aren't being provided

b) haven't provided

c) hadn't been provided

71. Why … to the list?

a) has it adding

b) has it been added

c) had it being added

72. Don't worry. Your knowledge … enough.

a) are

b) has

c) will be

73. How long … together?

a) have you being worked

b) have you been working

c) had you been working

74. She was exhausted. She … hard all morning.

a) had been working

b) had work

c) has been working

75. If Mary had passed the test, her parents … much happier.

a) would had been

b) would have been

c) might had been

76. If only I … more time!

a) have

b) did

c) had

77. Choose the correct sentence:

a) You don't have to overwork.

b) You don't need be overwork.

c) You didn't needed overwork.

78. It … much better.

a) would to be

b) would been

c) would have been

79. This name is familiar … me.

a) to

b) about

c) with

80. You need to be more polite … your customers.

a) of

b) to

c) on

81. He couldn't hear her. She shouted … him again.

a) to

b) of

c) towards

82. I agree with you … some extent.

a) of

b) on

c) to

83. They … this place by ten.

a) will leave

b) will be left

c) will have left

84. The manager said: "I'm busy now.".

a) The manager said that he was busy now.

b) The manager said that he has been busy then.

c) The manager said that he was busy then.

85. She asked me: "Do you agree?".

a) She asked me if I agreed.

b) She asked me I agreed

c) She asked me if had I agreed.

86. My friends asked me: "Where is this place?".

a) My friends asked me where was that place.

b) My friends asked me where that place was.

c) My friends asked me where that place has been.

87. She asked me: "How are your parents doing?".

a) She asked me how my parents were doing.

b) She asked me how my parents are doing.

c) She asked me how have been doing.

88. Choose the correct sentence:

a) Won't you hurrying up?

b) Didn't you hurried up?

c) Won't you hurry up?

89. Choose the correct sentence:

a) Isn't it getting more and more expensive?

b) Is not it getting more and more expensive?

c) Doesn't it getting more and more expensively?

90. I was … by the latest news regarding the war.

a) shocking

b) shocked

c) shockingly

91. Food prices have been … steadily for at least ten years.

a) rising

b) lifting

c) raising

92. I'll have to study hard, … I can pass the exam.

a) so that

b) such

c) in order

93. You … to eat if you are not hungry.

a) needn't

b) haven't

c) don't have

94. We'll dance and … we'll have lunch.

a) straight away

b) so

c) then

95. She has to go to Germany for the next … of the training.

a) step

b) stage

c) point

96. When the meeting had finished, we went … the plan once again.

a) up

b) down   c) over

97. I locked the animals in the cage to … them from getting away.

a) avoid   b) hinder

c) prevent

98. You're … your time trying to persuade her.

a) wasting   b) losing

c) missing

99. Our last cook was better than our … one.

a) latter   b) instant

c) current

100. I am grateful to Mary for being so patient … us.

a) for

b) with

c) at

101. Have you exchanged that lovely car … this?

a) with b) by   c) for

102. The weather was … the poor harvest.

a) condemned for

b) found fault with for

c) blamed for

103. Olivia is teaching three classes and she is examining at a literature exam tomorrow. …, she is chairing a meeting at the Bright Owl Club.

a) On top of it

b) At top

c) On the top of it

104. I don't see any … in arriving early at the show.

a) cause   b) point

c) reason

Answer Key

01.a 02.b 03.b 04.c

05.b 06.a 07.b 08.a 09.c 10.b 11.b 12.b 13.a 14.c 15.a 16.a 17.a 18.b 19.c

20.c 21.a 22.b 23.a 24.c 25.c 26.a 27.b 28.c 29.a 30.b 31.b 32.c 33.a 34.c

35.b 36.a 37.c 38.b 39.a 40.b 41.c 42.b 43.a 44.c 45.c 46.a 47.b 48.a 49.c

50.a 51.c 52.a 53.b 54.b 55.a 56.c 57.b 58.b 59.c 60.b 61.b 62.a 63.c 64.b

65.b 66.c 67.a 68.a 69.b 70.a 71.b 72.c 73.b 74.a 75.b 76.c 77.a 78.c 79.a

80.b 81.a 82.c 83.c 84.c 85.a 86.b 87.a 88.c 89.a 90.b 91.a 92.a 93.c 94.c

95.b 96.c 97.c 98.a 99.c 100.b

101.c 102.c 103.a 104.b

3. Test Paper II

01. The woman felt so … .
a) insecure   b) securing   c) asecure
02. The detectives will look … the crime.
a) in
b) with
c) into
03. My wife often shows … . She likes attracting other people's attention.
a) off
b) in
c) about
04. … no use doing it.
a) How's
b) There's
c) What's
05. There is no point … it again.
a) to check
b) about check
c) in checking
06. I have difficulty … for this exam.
a) to prepare
b) preparing
c) prepared
07. This competitor is expected.
a) to lose
b) losing
c) lose
08. It should … .
a) be say
b) be said
c) being said
09. These conditions should … .
a) be provided
b) providing
c) provide
10. The more practice, … .
a) better
b) the best
c) the better
11. She won't change unless her parents … to her.
a) talk
b) will talk
c) had talked
12. When his mother arrived, he … .
a) has been sleeping
b) would be sleeping
c) was still sleeping
13. … the manager explaining it?
a) Had
b) Was
c) Did
14. Is the following sentence correct? "What was she wanting?"
a) correct
b) incorrect

15. Is the following sentence correct? "The girls were commenting."
a) correct
b) incorrect
16. Is the following sentence correct? "I was parking there."
a) correct
b) incorrect
17. Is the following sentence correct? "Brian was having a rest."
a) correct
b) incorrect
18. Choose the correct sentence:
a) I was never to China.
b) I've never been to China.
c) I'd never been to China.
19. You brother has … the last place.
a) be taken
b) been taken
c) taken
20. Olivia … it for six years.
a) had been doing
b) has been doing
c) would be done
21. … her since you finished university?
a) Have you known
b) Have you been knowing
c) Did you known

22. Choose the correct sentence:
a) Did it ever been controlled?
b) Had it ever being controlled?
c) Has it ever been controlled?

23. Her mistakes … .
a) did be spotted
b) have been spotted
c) had being spotted
24. I observed that his mistakes … yet.
a) weren't corrected
b) didn't be correct
c) hadn't been corrected
25. I … it two months ago.
a) have done
b) done
c) did
26. How long … there?
a) are you staying
b) have you been staying
c) did you being stay
27. My sister … Russian for three years.
a) has been learning
b) had been learning
c) did learning
28. Choose the correct sentence:
a) It is currently monitored.
b) It had currently be monitored.
c) It is currently being monitored.
29. I found out that some things … .
a) had been stolen
b) were stolen
c) did be stolen
30. The students is frightened … her words.
a) of

b) with

c) on

31. She's ashamed … her poor skills.
a) by
b) on
c) of

32. This text was translated from Russian … German.
a) into
b) with
c) on

33. Why is he staring … her?
a) on
b) at
c) to

34. I'm working here … the time being.
a) for
b) at
c) in

35. The analyst said: "The situation isn't getting better.".
a) The analyst said that the situation isn't getting better.
b) The analyst said that the situation wasn't getting better.
c) The analyst said that the situation wouldn't get better.

36. The manager said: "They were discussing it.".
a) The manager said that they had been discussing it.
b) The manager said that they were discussing it.
c) The manager said that they would be discussing it.

37. The secretary asked me: "Did he apologize for it?".
a) The secretary asked me if he apologized for it.
b) The secretary asked me if he has apologized for it.
c) The secretary asked me if he had apologized for it.

38. Mary asked me: "Has she already introduced him?".
a) Mary asked me if she had already introduced him.
b) Mary asked me if she already introduced him.
c) Mary asked me if she would already introduce him.

39. Kate asked me: "What time do you usually get up?".
a) Kate asked me what time did I usually get up.
b) Kate asked me what time had I usually got up.
c) Kate asked me what time I usually got up.

40. The manager asked me: "Who was responsible for it?".
a) The manager asked me who had been responsible for it.
b) The manager asked me who was responsible for it.
c) The manager asked me who has be responsible for it.

41. The girl asked me: "How often will you go to the gym?".
a) The girl asked me how often I will go to the gym.

b) The girl asked me how often
I would go to the gym.
c) The girl asked me how often I
used to go to the gym.
42. My neighbour asked me:
"Why were you doing it all
night?".
a) My neighbour asked me why
you had been doing it all night.
b) My neighbour asked me why
I had been doing it all night.
c) My neighbour asked me why
have I been doing it all night.
43. Choose the correct sentence:
a) Hadn't it improve your
English?
b) Doesn't it improve your
English?
c) Haven't it improving your
English?
44. … she trust you?
a) Doesn't
b) Isn't
c) Hadn't
45. … she lose control?
a) Wasn't
b) Hadn't
c) Didn't
46. Choose the correct answer:
a) Hasn't Dave become a rich
man?
b) Didn't Dave became a rich
man?
c) Hadn't Dave been became a
rich man?
47. …, it ruined all our hopes.
a) Luck

b) Iluckily
c) Unluckily
48. Maria feels so … .
Something bad must have
happened to her.
a) unhappy
b) unhappily
c) happily
49. This … isn't enough to enter
our organization.
a) unknown
b) knowledge
c) knowing
50. He's an … person. He's so
special!
a) ordinarily
b) ordinary
c) extraordinary
51. Her father ran … when she
was a small kid.
a) off
b) in
c) out
52. We'll sort … this problem
quite easily.
a) in
b) about
c) out
53. I can't get rid … my
headache.
a) on
b) of
c) out
54. She always stands … in a
crowd.
a) within
b) out

c) about

55. We broke … all the relations.
a) off
b) out
c) to

56. You … better change your mind.
a) can
b) had
c) would

57. I … my hair cut.
a) can
b) should
c) had

58. This thing can be … .
a) proved
b) proving
c) prove

59. The team shouldn't … .
a) divide
b) be divided
c) diving

60. It's … fantastic what you've done.
a) completely
b) utter
c) such a

61. We won't go there in case she … buy a ticket.
a) won't
b) doesn't
c) wouldn't

62. How … it changing?
a) did
b) have

c) was

63. It … an effect on me.
a) won't have
b) hadn't have
c) wouldn't had

64. The police … suspected Mary.
a) have
b) has
c) did

65. They … broken the law. I guarantee.
a) didn't
b) haven't
c) won't

66. The customer … responded.
a) won't
b) didn't
c) hasn't

67. She … the money.
a) withdrew
b) withdrawed
c) withdraw

68. She realized she … inappropriate words.
a) was used
b) had used
c) did used

69. They … now.
a) be criticized
b) are criticize
c) are being criticized

70. What … now?
a) is being said
b) has being said
c) does been said

71. Who … about this situation?
a) did been warned
b) has been warned
c) would being warned

72. How long … this movie?
a) did you watched
b) hadn't you watch
c) have you been watching

73. Jennifer confessed she …
him all the truth.
a) didn't told
b) won't tell
c) hadn't told

74. I wish I … a better job.
a) had
b) would had
c) have

75. I … be in best shape because
it's my desire to be so.
a) must
b) have to
c) had to

76. I … to finish this report
today.
a) have to
b) had to
c) would have

77. The professor told me:
"We'll support her.".
a) The professor told me that
they will support her.
b) The professor told me that
they would support her.
c) The professor told me that
they would be supporting her.

78. I … my final exam by
December.
a) will completed
b) will be completing
c) will have completed

79. We … for two hours by the
time they arrive.
a) will have been talking
b) will had been talked
c) will had been talking

80. The assistant asked me:
"Will you compare their
results?".
a) The assistant asked me
whether I would compare their
results.
b) The assistant asked me if I
will compare their results.
c) The assistant asked me if I
would be comparing their
results.

81. The professor asked me:
"Have you been learning
Russian for three
years?".
a) The professor asked me if
you had been learning Russian
for three years.
b) The professor asked me if I
had been learning Russian for
three
years.
c) The professor asked me if I
have learnt Russian for three
years.

82. My cousin asked me: "How
was your trip?".

a) My cousin asked me how my trip was.
b) My cousin asked me how my trip had been.
c) My cousin asked me how my trip would be.
83. What does Jane insist …?
a) of   b) with c) on
84. Her colleagues … her.
a) disrespect   b) inrespect
c) arespect
85. He's my … .
a) competition
b) competitive
c) competitor
86. The coronavirus can't be cured … .
a) traditional
b) traditionally
c) tradition
87. She improved her Chinese only … .
a) unsignificantly
b) insignificantly
c) dissignificantly
88. We lead an … lifestyle.
a) inhealthy
b) dishealthy
c) unhealthy
89. They are very … to him.
a) unkind
b) inkind
c) rekind
90. Brian dozed ... during the lecture.
a) down   b) in
c) off

91. Choose the correct sentence:
a) Get out it your head!
b) Get it out of your head!
c) Get out of your head it!
92. Choose the correct sentence:
a) I'm accustomed to staying at home all day.
b) I'm accustomed to stay at home all day.
c) I'm accustom to staying at home all day.
93. I'd rather … cycling than play computer games.
a) going
b) gone
c) go
94. I'd rather … a little bit.
a) wait b) waiting c) to wait
95. She's supposed … the first place.
a) take b) to take
c) to have take
96. Are we supposed … there on time?
a) arrive
b) arriving
c) to arrive
97. These risk factors should .
a) minimize
b) minimizing
c) be minimized
98. This subject shouldn't … at university.
a) teach
b) be taught
c) teaching
99. They mustn't … .

a) punished

b) punishing

c) be punished

c) The shortest

100. …, the better.

a) The shorter

b) Shorter

Answer Key

01.a 02.c 03.a 04.b

05.c 06.b 07.a 08.b 09.a 10.c 11.a 12.c 13.b

14.b 15.a 16.a 17.a 18.b 19.c 20.b 21.a 22.c

23.b 24.c 25.c 26.b 27.a 28.c 29.a 30.a 31.c

32.a 33.b 34.a 35.b 36.a 37.c 38.a 39.c 40.a

41.b 42.b 43.b 44.a 45.c 46.a 47.c 48.a 49.b

50.c 51.a 52.c 53.b 54.b 55.a 56.b 57.c 58.a

59.b 60.a 61.b 62.c 63.a 64.a 65.b 66.c 67.a

68.b 69.c 70.a 71.b 72.c 73.c 74.a 75.a 76.a

77.b 78.c 79.a 80.a 81.b 82.b 83.c 84.a 85.c

86.b 87.b 88.c 89.a 90.c 91.b 92.a 93.c 94.a

95.b 96.c 97.c 98.b 99.c 100.a

4. Applied Grammar Rules

Use of Complements

Model I.—Many brave soldiers lost their lives in that war.

 Kind, a simple declarative sentence.
 Subject, soldiers.   Adj. modifiers of subj., many, brave.
 Predicate, lost.   Object, lives.
 Adj. modifier of obj., their.
 Adv. modifier of pred., in that war.

II: Still in thy right hand carry gentle peace to silence envious tongues.

 Kind, a simple imperative sentence.
 Subject, [you.]   Predicate, carry.
 Object, peace.   Adj. modifier of obj., gentle.
 Adv. modifiers of pred., still, in thy right hand, to silence envious tongues.

III. Haing crossed the river, he ran into the adjoining wood.

Kind, a simple declarative sentence.
Subject, he.
Participial mod. of subj., having crossed the river.
Predicate, ran.
Adv. mod. of pred., into the adjoining wood.

IV: My pupils like to write stories.

 Kind, a simple declarative sentence.
 Subject, pupils.   Adj. mod. of subj., my.

Predicate, like.　　　　Object, to write stories.
Object of to write, stories.

V: The scholars gave their teacher a beautiful present.

Kind, a simple declarative sentence.
Subject, scholars.　　　　Adj. mod. of subj., the.
Predicate, gave.　　　　Direct object, present.

Adj. modifiers of direct obj., a, beautiful.
Indirect object, teacher.　　　　Adj. mod. of indirect obj., their.

VI: It is wrong to slight your work.

Kind, a simple declarative sentence.
Real subject, to slight your work.
Representative subject, it.
Predicate, { Verb of incomplete predication, is.
　　　　{ Adj. <u>complement</u>[1] of predicate, wrong.

EXERCISES

1.　　　My father gave me a fine pony.
2.　　　At this moment the noise grew louder.
3.　　　There are eight girls in the class.
4.　　　Seek the company of the good.
5.　　　It is a sin to deceive anyone.
6.　　　How could he mark thee for the silent tomb!
7.　　　Crossing the field, I found a knife, rusty and broken.
8.　　　On an eminence above the sea paces a strong, rough
Cornishman.
9.　　　On the eastern side of the Nile lies the temple of Karnak.
10.　　　For their lean country much disdain,
We English often show.

---

[1] *When the predicate is completed by an adjunct describing the subject, the completing adjunct is called the complement.*

11.   Home they brought her warrior dead.—Tennyson.

12.   Bright-eyed beauty once was she.—Lucy Larcom.

13.   Do men gather figs from thorns?—Bible.

14.   The lowing herd winds slowly o'er the lea.—Gray.

15.   These are the gardens of the desert.—Bryant.

16.   Soon on the hill's steep verge he stood.—Scott.

17.   The Indian knows his place of rest far in the cedar shade.—
Hemans.

18.   Through all eternity, to Thee A joyful song I'll raise.—Addison.

19.   The uncertain vacillating temper common to all Indians now
began to declare itself.—Parkman.

20.   The fine English cavalry then advanced to support their archers,
and to attack the Scottish line.—Scott.

21.   So saying, from the ruined shrine he stept.—Tennyson.

22.   Yet Fortune was bending over him, just ready to let fall a burden
of gold.—Hawthorne.

23.   On the first day of his fasting,
Through the leafy woods he wandered.—Longfellow.

24.   Raising his head, he looked the lustrous stranger in the face.—
Hawthorne.

25.   At daybreak on the bleak sea-beach,
A fisherman stood aghast, To see the form of a maiden fair
Lashed close to a drifting mast.—Longfellow.

26.   Well had the boding tremblers learned to trace
The day's disasters in his morning face.—Goldsmith.

27.   All the livelong day, Oliver paced softly up and down the
garden, raising his eyes every instant to the sick chamber, and
shuddering to see the darkened window.—Dickens.

28.   By Nebo's lonely mountain, On this side Jordan's wave,
In a vale in the land of Moab,   There lies a lonely grave.—Mrs.
Alexander.

29.   Wolfe had discovered a narrow path winding up the side of the
steep precipice from the river.—Warburton.

30.   Along the cool sequestered vale of life
They kept the noiseless tenor of their way.—Gray.

31.   The silent influence of Shakespeare's poetry on millions of young hearts in England, in Germany, in all the world, shows the almost superhuman power of human genius.—Müller.

32.   Now see him mounted once again Upon his nimble steed, Full slowly pacing o'er the stones, With caution and good heed.—Cowper.

33.   By comparing the words of these inscriptions with many others, the proper method of interpreting this peculiar language was ascertained.—Ontario Reader.

34.   Failing in this, they set themselves, after their custom on such occasions, to building a rude fort of their own in the neighboring forest.—Parkman.

35.   I heard a brooklet gushing

From its rocky fountain near,

Down into the valley rushing,

So fresh and wondrous clear.—Longfellow.

36.   Up from the meadows rich with corn,

Clear in the cool September morn, The clustered spires of Frederick stand Green-walled by the hills of Maryland.—Whittier.

37.   No nightingale did ever chant So sweetly to reposing bands Of Travellers in some shady haunt Among Arabian sands.—Wordsworth.

38.   The French, blown and exhausted, inferior beside in weight both of man and horse, offered but a short resistance.—Lever.

39.   Looking, looking for the mark,

Down the others came,

Struggling through the snowdrifts stark,

Calling out his name.—Lushington.

40.   A voice so thrilling ne'er was heard

In spring-time from the Cuckoo bird,

Breaking the silence of the seas

Among the farthest Hebrides.—Wordsworth.

.

Use of Clauses

Clauses[2] may be principal[3], subordinate[4] type. It may take the role of noun[5], adjective[6] or adverb[7].

Select the principal clauses and the subordinate clauses in the following sentences, and state the function of each subordinate clause:—

1.	They knew who did it.
2.	The book which you gave me, is here.
3.	I shall go when he returns.

A noun clause may be used:—

1.As the object of a verb; as, He knew what I did.

2.As the subject of a verb; as, What course he pursued is seen now.

3.As the object of a preposition; as, My friend annoyed me by what he said.

4.As a predicate nominative; as, The end of it all is (that) he receives his choice.

---

[2] *A clause is a group of words that forms part of a sentence and that contains a subject and a predicate. A clause used as a part of speech is called a subordinate clause. All other clauses are said to be independent.*

Clauses of the same order or rank are said to be coördinate.
Sentences may be simple, compound, or complex.
1. A simple sentence has but one subject and one predicate, either or both of which may be compound.
2. A compound sentence consists of two or more independent coördinate clauses, which may or may not be joined by conjunctions.
3. A complex sentence consists of two or more clauses, one of which is independent and the rest subordinate.
A compound sentence in which one or more of the coördinate clauses are complex is called a compound complex sentence.

[3] *The leading thought of a sentence is called the principal clause.*
[4] *A clause that has the function of a noun, an adjective, or an adverb, is called a subordinate clause.*
[5] *A clause that has the function of a noun, is called a noun clause; as, He said he knew his lesson. How I shall reach my destination is the question.*
[6] *A clause that has the use or function of an adjective, is called an adjective clause; as, He found the book which he lost.*
[7] *A clause that has the use or function of an adverb, is called an adverbial clause; as, I shall go where they are. He will destroy it unless we hinder him.*

Depending upon combination of clauses in a sentence we have <u>complex</u>[8] and <u>compound</u>[9] sentences. A compound sentence that is made up of complex sentences, or simple and complex sentences, is called a compound-complex sentence; as, We entered the building, and a man who was working there, gave us information about it.

EXERCISES.

Name the clauses in the following sentences, and state the kind and relation (if any) of each:—
1. Whilst I was thus musing, I cast my eyes towards the summit of a rock that was not far from me, where I discovered one in the habit of a shepherd, with a musical instrument in his hand.—Addison.

Model.—
Whilst . . . . musing is an adv. clause, mod. cast.
I cast . . . . a rock is a principal clause.
That . . . . . me is an adj. clause, mod. summit of a rock.
Where I . . . hand is an adj. clause, mod. summit of a rock.
2. King Harold had a rebel brother in Flanders, who was a vassal of Harold Hardrada, king of Norway.—Dickens.

3. Those who knew him best affirmed that this Mr. Toil was a very worthy character, and that he had done more good, both to children and grown people, than anybody else in the world.—Hawthorne.

4. Portia, when she returned, was in that happy temper of mind which never fails to attend the consciousness of having performed a good action; her cheerful spirits enjoyed everything she saw: the moon never seemed to shine so brightly before; and when that pleasant moon was hid behind a cloud, then a light which she saw from her house at Belmont as well pleased her charmed fancy.—Lamb.

---

[8] *A sentence that consists of one principal clause, and one or more subordinate clauses, is called a complex sentence; as, I have met the person of whom you speak.*
[9] *A sentence that consists of two or more independent clauses, is called a compound sentence; as, James came home, but John remained there.*

5. Once upon a time, there lived a very rich man, and a king besides, whose name was Midas; and he had a little daughter, whom nobody but himself ever heard of, and whose name I either never knew, or have entirely forgotten. So, because I love odd names for little girls, I choose to call her Marygold.—Hawthorne.

6. I rose and prepared to leave the Abbey. As I descended the flight of steps which lead into the body of the building, my eye was caught by the shrine of Edward the Confessor, and I ascended the small staircase that conducts to it, to take from thence a general survey of this wilderness of tombs.—Irving.

7. All things that love the sun are out of doors;
The sky rejoices in the morning's birth;
The grass is bright with rain-drops;—on the moors
The hare is running races in her mirth.—Wordsworth.

8. I thought of a mound in sweet Auburn
Where a little headstone stood;
How the flakes were folding it gently,
As did robins the babes in the wood.—Lowell.

9. Lightly they'll talk of the spirit that's gone,
And o'er his cold ashes upbraid him;
But little he'll reck if they let him sleep on
In the grave where a Briton has laid him.—Wolfe.

10. The humble boon was soon obtained;
The Aged Minstrel audience gained.
But, when he reached the room of state,
Where she, with all her ladies, sate,
Perchance he wished his boon denied:
For when to tune his harp he tried,
His trembling hand had lost the ease
Which marks security to please.—Scott.

Use of Should or would!

When the auxiliary verb expresses futurity without any idea of wishing, consenting, or the like, the forms are as follows:—

Assertions (Declarative)

SINGULAR	PLURAL
1. I should fall.	1. We should fall.
2. Thou wouldst fall.	2. You would fall.
3. He would fall.	3. They would fall.

Questions (Interrogative)

SINGULAR	PLURAL
1. Should I fall?	1. Should we fall?
2. Shouldst thou fall?	2. Should you fall?
3. Would he fall?	3. Would they fall?

Examples: Use should or would ……
1. Should you drown if the boat were to capsize? [Yes, I should drown, for I do not know how to swim.]
2. Should you despair if this plan were a failure? [No, I should not, for I have other resources.]
3. Should you think that ten yards of velvet would be enough? [Yes, I should think so.]
4. Should you be offended if I were to speak frankly? [No, I should not be offended.]
5. Should you wish to examine the plans again before deciding? [Yes, I should (see note under I, above).]
6. Would you wear a hat or a cap? [I would wear a cap if I were you.]
7. Would you study Greek if you were in my place? [Yes, I would.]
8. Would you accept my apology if it were offered? [Certainly, I would accept it gladly.]
9. Would you be so kind as to lend me your compasses? [Certainly I would lend them, if I had not lost them.]
10. Would you allow me to use your name as a reference? [I would.]
11. I should break my neck if I fell.
12. I should hesitate to try this experiment.

13. I shouldn't wonder if he escaped.

14. We should regret any misunderstanding.

15. I should wish to examine the plans again before deciding.

16. I should be glad to accept any fair offer.

17. I would give five dollars for a ticket.

18. I would help you if I could.

19. I would never agree to such a proposition.

20. We would rather die than surrender.

21. What would happen if {I | you | he} should not carry out the commander's instructions?

22. If {I | you | he} should miss the steamer, our friends would be alarmed.

23. Whoever {shall | should} violate this law {shall | should} pay the penalty. [That is: If anybody shall violate, etc.]

24. Whenever {I | you | he} shall find an opportunity, let us try the experiment. [That is: If ever I shall find, etc.]

25. He promised to assist you whenever you should need help. [Whenever = if ever.]

26. Though {we | you | they} should fail, others would make the attempt. [Concession.]

27. Though Evans should disappoint me, I should not lose confidence in him.

28. Vernon will do his part if {I | you | they} will coöperate with him.

29. If {I | you | he} will only make the effort, success is certain.

30. Edmund would reveal the secret if {I | you | they} would assist him in his search for the treasure.

31. If we would take pains, our parents would be satisfied.

32. Whoever will join us may be sure of a pleasant and profitable journey. [That is: If any one will join us, he may be sure, etc.]

33. We would pay our bill to-day if we had the money.

34. I would gladly accept any fair offer.

35. Templeton insists that you shall accompany him.

     This letter directs where you shall station yourself.

     We gave orders that the gates should be closed.[10]

---

[10] *Shall and should are often used in the second and third persons in subordinate clauses to express volition which is not that of the subject.*

Use of Infinitive

An infinitive may be modified by an adverb, an adverbial phrase, or an adverbial clause.

To write legibly is a valuable accomplishment.

It would be useless to search longer.

They allowed him to go in peace. [Adverbial phrase.]

To dive among those weeds would be folly.

Theodore promises to come when I send for him. [Adverbial clause.]

No modifier should be inserted between to and the infinitive.

I beg you to inquire carefully into this matter. [Not: to carefully inquire.]

Mr. Harris moved to postpone the question indefinitely. [Not: to indefinitely postpone.]

I expect always to be poor. [Not: to always be poor.]

The infinitive may take an object if its meaning allows.

I long to visit Italy.My mother feared to enter the house. To launch a boat was impossible. To grant your request is a pleasure. To give him money is useless. [Money is the direct object of to give, and him the indirect object.]

An infinitive with or without a complement or modifiers, may be used as the subject of a sentence, as a predicate nominative, or as an appositive.

To descend was extremely difficult. [Subject.]

To secure a seat was impossible.

To sing well requires practice.

His delight was to travel. [Predicate nominative.]

The governor's policy is to wait.

My wish is to see you immediately.

To decide was to act. [The first infinitive is the subject, and the second is a predicate nominative.]

Both alternatives, to advance and to retreat, seemed equally hazardous. [Apposition with the subject.]

My first plan, to tunnel under the wall, proved a failure.

He has but one aim in life, to succeed. [Apposition with the object.]

I have written with a definite purpose, to dissuade you.

I give you three choices,—to buy, to lease, or to build.

[in apposition with the expletive subject it.]
It was a pleasure to see him. [Instead of: To see him was a pleasure.]
It is easy to understand you.
It will be impossible to forget.
It proved very difficult to find evidence against him

[As the object of the prepositions but, except, about.]
There was nothing to do but walk (or to walk).
He will do anything except resign (or except to resign).
We are about to object. [An idiom expressing futurity.]
The train is about to start..
Rikin is about to speak the truth about incidents of last night.

Use of infinitive as modifier[11]

WITH NOUNS (ADJECTIVE MODIFIER)	WITH ADJECTIVES (ADVERBIAL MODIFIER)
An opportunity *to advance* came.	The men are *ready to advance*.
Determination *to win* brings success.	John is eager *to win*.
Willingness *to oblige* makes friends.	I shall be glad *to oblige* you.
I wish I had the ability *to swim*.	We are all able *to swim*.
His anxiety *to please* us was laughable.	He is anxious *to please* everybody.

A predicate pronoun after to be in an infinitive clause is in the objective case, agreeing with the subject of the infinitive. Use of relatives relatives and of the predicate pronouns in the following sentences:—

---

[11] *"determination to win" is equivalent to "determination for victory," and "eager to win" to "eager for victory." The adjective force of the infinitive comes out clearly in "nothing to eat," where to eat is practically synonymous with eatable.*
In its adjective use, the present infinitive sometimes shows no distinction in voice, so that the active and the passive are interchangeable: as,—"a house to let" or "to be let"; "an axe to grind" or "to be ground." In such expressions the active form is usually preferable.

A boy whom I thought to be honest deceived me. [Whom is the subject of the infinitive to be and is therefore in the objective case.]
A boy who, I thought, was honest deceived me. [Who is the subject of was and is therefore nominative. I thought is parenthetical]
A boy whom I believe to be him just passed me.
A boy who, I believe, was he, just passed me.

PREDICATE PRONOUN AFTER *TO BE*	PREDICATE NOMINATIVE
I believed it to be *her*.	I believed that it was *she*.
We know the author to be *him*.	We know that the author is *he*.
	The author is known to be *he*.
He thought Richard to be *me*.	He thought that Richard was *I*.
	Richard was thought to be *I*.
We suspected the intruders to be *them*.	We suspected that the intruders were *they*.

Use of relative and predicative pronouns:

A boy whom I thought to be honest deceived me.
[Whom is the subject of the infinitive to be and is therefore in the objective case.]
A boy who, I thought, was honest deceived me. [Who is the subject of was and is therefore nominative. I thought is parenthetical]
A boy whom I believe to be honest just passed me.
A boy who, I believe, was Rikin, just passed me.
A lady who, I thought, was sincere at her job sites deceived me.

Use of infinitive clause with for[12]:
For us to delay would be fatal to your enterprise. [Compare: Our delay would be fatal.]
Our best plan is for the boat to shoot the rapids. [Predicate nominative agreeing with the subject plan.]

---

[12] *Infinitive clause with for may be used as a subject, as a predicate nominative, or as the object of a preposition.*

I see no way out of the difficulty except for them to offer an apology. [Compare: except the offer of an apology on their part.]

Use of Participle[13]:

Who thundering comes on blackest steed?—Byron.

Clinging to the horns of the altar, voiceless she stood.—De Quincey.

Deserted, surrounded, outnumbered, and with everything at stake, he did not even deign to stand on the defensive.—Macaulay.

Shrouded in such baleful vapors, the genius of Burns was never seen in clear azure splendor, enlightening the world.—Carlyle.

Past Participle of a weak verb.

PRESENT TENSE	PAST TENSE	PAST PARTICIPLE
I *mend* chairs.	I *mended* the chairs.	The chairs are *mended*.
I *sweep* the rooms.	I *swept* the rooms.	The rooms are *swept*.
I *seek* treasure.	I *sought* treasure.	Treasure is *sought*.
I *lose* money.	I *lost* money.	The money is *lost*.

Past Participle of a strong verb

PRESENT TENSE	PAST TENSE	PAST PARTICIPLE
He *speaks*.	He *spoke*.	(He has) *spoken*.
He *draws*.	He *drew*.	(He has) *drawn*.
He *sings*.	He *sang*.	(He has) *sung*.
He *wins*.	He *won*.	(He has) *won*.

A participle should not be used without some substantive to which it may belong.

Right: Entering the room, we saw a strange sight. [The participle entering belongs to the pronoun we.]

Wrong: Entering the room, a strange sight was seen. [Since there is no substantive to which entering can belong, it has no construction.]

---

[13] *The participle is a verb-form which has no subject, but which partakes of the nature of an adjective and expresses action or state in such a way as to describe or limit a substantive.*

A participle may be modified by an adverb, an adverbial phrase, or an adverbial clause.

Smiling brightly, she extended her hand. [Adverb.]

He leaped forward, shrieking with all his might. [Adverbial phrase.]

Laughing until he cried, he sank into a chair. [Adverbial clause.]

A participle may be used as a pure adjective.

A grinning boy confronted me. A battered hat hung on the peg.

Kate was playing with a broken doll. We could hear a rushing stream.

Willing hands make light work. He was struck by a spent ball.

Use of substantive with a participle[14]:

My knife slipping, I cut myself severely. [The phrase my knife slipping is equivalent to because my knife slipped: it expresses cause.]

Two days having elapsed, we again set forward. [The phrase in italics is equivalent to when two days had elapsed: it expresses time.]

Evenings he read aloud, his wife sewing by his side. [The phrase expresses one of the circumstances that attended the reading.]

This done, proceed to business. [The phrase this done is equivalent to the clause since (or when) this is done, and indicates cause or time.]

Uses of noun clauses[15]:

That Milton was spared has often caused surprise. [Subject.]

Brutus said that Cæsar was a tyrant. [Object of said.]

Cæsar commanded that the prisoners should be spared. [Object.]

I wish that you would work harder. [Object.]

The traveller inquired where he could find the inn. [Object.]

He asked me what my name was. [Second object of asked.]

My fear that the bridge might fall proved groundless. [Apposition with fear.]

One fact is undoubted,—that the state of America has been kept in continual agitation.—Burke. [Apposition with fact.]

---

[14] *A substantive, with a participle, may express the cause, time, or circumstances of an action. This is called the absolute construction. The substantive is in the nominative case and is called a nominative absolute.*

[15] *(1) as subject, (2) as direct object of a transitive verb, (3) in apposition with a substantive, (4) as a predicate nominative.*

Noun Clauses

Usefulness of the noun clause in its various constructions.

1. That the king would ever again have received Becket into favor is not to be believed.—Southey.

2. That in education we should proceed from the simple to the complex is a truth which has always been to some extent acted on.—Spencer.

3. How great his reputation was, is proved by the embassies sent to him.—Coleridge.

4. It vexed old Hawkins that his counsel was not followed.—Fuller.

5. It became necessary, at last, that I should arouse both master and valet to the expediency of removing the treasure.—Poe.

6. There is no doubt that breeds may be made as different as species in many physiological characteristics.—Huxley.

7. The main definition you could give of old Marquis Mirabeau is, that he was of the pedant species.—Carlyle.

8. The fact seems to be that we have survived the tremendous explosion.—Brougham.

9. The question is, whether the feigned image of poesy, or the regular instruction of philosophy, have the more force in teaching.—Sidney.

10. I feared that some serious disaster had befallen my friend.—Poe.

11. I think with you that the most magnificent object under heaven is the great deep.—Cowper.

12. Aureolus soon discovered that the success of his artifices had only raised up a more determined adversary.—Gibbon.

13. Harold alleged that he was appointed by Edward.—Temple.

14. That we shall die, we know.—Shakspere.

15. Her Majesty has promised that the treaty shall be laid before her Parliament.—Swift.

16. Deerslayer proposed that they should circle the point in the canoe.—Cooper.

17. I remembered how soft was the hand of Sleep.—Landor.

18. I cannot see what objection can justly be made to the practice.—Reynolds.

19. No man knew what was to be expected from this strange tribunal.—Macaulay.

20. We may imagine with what sensations the stupefied Spaniards must have gazed on this horrid spectacle.—Prescott.

21. Observe how graciously Nature instructs her human children.—Coleridge.

22. My friend asked me if there would not be some danger in coming home late.—Addison.

23. A message came that the committee was sitting at Kensington Palace.—Thackeray.

24. Jeffreys had obtained of the king a promise that he would not pardon her.—Burnet.

25. The present age seems pretty well agreed in an opinion that the utmost scope and end of reading is amusement only.—Fielding.

26. He suddenly alarmed me by a startling question—whether I had seen the show of prize cattle that morning in Smithfield.—Lamb.

27. I am told that the Lancashire system is perfect.—Kingsley.

Correct use of shall and will, should and would, in the indirect discourse:—

1. He writes me that he believes he shall be at Eton till the middle of November.—Gray. [Direct: I shall be at Eton.]

2. He that would pass the latter part of his life with honor and decency, must, while he is young, consider that he shall one day be old.—Johnson. [Direct: I shall one day be old.]

3. Could he but reduce the Aztec capital, he felt that he should be safe.—Prescott. [Direct: I shall be safe.]

4. Plantagenet took it into his head that he should like to learn to play at bowls.—Disraeli. [Direct: I should like.]

5. He answered that he should be very proud of hoisting his flag under Sir John's command.—Southey. [Direct: I shall (or should) be, etc.]

6. He knew that if he applied himself in earnest to the work of reformation, he should raise every bad passion in arms against him.—Macaulay. [Direct: If I apply myself ..., I shall raise, etc.]

7. He was pleased to say that he should like to have the author in his service.—Carlyle. [Direct: I should like.]

8. Mr. Tristram at last declared that he was overcome with fatigue, and should be happy to sit down.—Henry James. [Direct: I should be happy.]

9. She vowed that unless he made a great match, she should never die easy.—Thackeray. [Direct: Unless you make a great match, I shall never die easy.]

10. You think now I shall get into a scrape at home. You think I shall scream and plunge and spoil everything.—George Eliot. [Direct: She will get into a scrape, etc.]

11. You in a manner impose upon them the necessity of being silent, by declaring that you will be so yourself.—Cowper. [Determination: I will be silent.]

12. He [Swift] tells them that he will run away and leave them, if they do not instantly make a provision for him.—Jeffrey. [Threat: I will run away.]

13. The king declared that he would not reprieve her for one day.—Mackintosh. [Direct: I will not.]

14. Horace declares that he would not for all the world get into a boat with a man who had divulged the Eleusinian mysteries.—Cowper. [Direct: I would not.]

15. I called up Sirboko, and told him, if he would liberate this one man to please me, he should be no loser.—Speke. [Direct: If you will liberate, etc., you shall be no loser.]

16. We concluded that, if we did not come at some water in ten days' time, we would return.—De Foe. [Direct: If we do not, etc., we will return.]

17. With a theatrical gesture and the remark that I should see, he opened some cages and released half a dozen cats.—W. J. Locke. [Direct: You shall see.]

Modifiers

Modifiers of substantive complements:—

Herbert lost a gold watch. [The direct object (watch) is modified by the adjectives a and gold.]

The duke built towers of marble. [The direct object (towers) is modified by the adjective phrase of marble.]

My father built the house in which I was born. [The direct object (house) is modified by the adjective the and the adjective clause in which I was born.]

I saw a man running across the field. [The direct object (man) is modified by the adjective a and the participle running.]

You have forfeited your right to vote. [The direct object (right) is modified by the possessive pronoun your and the infinitive to vote.]

I have seen Henry's brother. [The direct object (brother) is modified by the possessive noun Henry's.]

I must ask my brother, the mayor. [The direct object (brother) is modified by the possessive pronoun my and the appositive mayor.]

The guild has elected Walter honorary president. [The predicate objective (president) is modified by the adjective honorary.]

Her husband is an old soldier. [The predicate nominative (soldier) is modified by the adjectives an and old.]

Her sons are veterans of the Franco-Prussian war. [The predicate nominative (veterans) is modified by the adjective phrase of the Franco-Prussian war.]

They are rivals in business. [The predicate nominative (rivals) is modified by the adjective phrase in business.]

The author is Will Jewell, who was formerly editor of "The Pioneer." [The predicate nominative (Will Jewell) is modified by the adjective clause who was formerly editor, etc.]

Baldwin is the man standing under the tree. [The predicate nominative (man) is modified by the adjective the and the participle standing.]

Your chief fault is your inclination to procrastinate. [The predicate nominative (inclination) is modified by the possessive pronoun your and the infinitive to procrastinate.]

This man is Gretchen's brother. [The predicate nominative (brother) is modified by the possessive noun Gretchen's.]
The first to fall was the bugler, John Wilson. [The predicate nominative (bugler) is modified by the adjective the and the appositive John Wilson.]

Construction of compound complex setences:
compound complex sentences are:—

1. The people drove out King Athamas, because he had killed his child; and he roamed about in his misery, till he came to the Oracle in Delphi.—Kingsley.
2. Society is the stage on which manners are shown; novels are their literature.—Emerson.
3. We keep no bees, but if I lived in a hive I should scarcely have more of their music.—Cowper.
4. The same river ran on as it had run on before, but the cheerful faces that had once been reflected in its stream had passed away.—Froude.
5. There are some laws and customs in this empire very peculiar; and if they were not so directly contrary to those of my own dear country, I should be tempted to say a little in their justification.—Swift.
6. Here they arrived about noon, and Joseph proposed to Adams that they should rest awhile in this delightful place.—Fielding.
7. I never saw a busier person than she seemed to be; yet it was difficult to say what she did.—C. Brontë.
8. Malaga possessed a brave and numerous garrison, and the common people were active, hardy, and resolute; but the city was rich and commercial, and under the habitual control of opulent merchants, who dreaded the ruinous consequences of a siege.—Irving.
9. The Spaniards were not to be taken by surprise; and, before the barbarian horde had come within their lines, they opened such a deadly fire from their heavy guns, supported by the musketry and crossbows, that the assailants were compelled to fall back slowly, but fearfully mangled, to their former position.—Prescott.
10. Her cheeks were as pale as marble, but of a cold, unhealthy, ashen white; and my heart ached to think that they had been bleached, most probably, by bitter and continual tears.—Hood.

11. The hawk, having in spiral motion achieved the upper flight, fell like a thunderbolt on the raven, stunned him with the blow, clutched him in his talons, folded him in his wings, and, the hawk undermost, they tumbled down like a black ball, till within a short distance from the earth.—Trelawny.

Use of Ellipsis[16]: …

In the following examples the omitted words are supplied in brackets.
[I] thank you.
[I] pray do not [you] move.
[You] pass me that book.
Her hair is light, her eyes [are] dark blue.
Some of the strangers spoke French, others [spoke] Spanish.
Some of the patriots were armed with old flintlocks, others [were armed] with swords, still others [were armed] with pitchforks.
When [he was] a youth, he travelled in the East.
Though [he is] timid, he is no coward.
They were amused, though [they were] somewhat vexed.
While [we were] drifting downstream, we grounded on a sand bar.
If [it is] possible, send me word to-night.
You shall have the money this week, if [it is] necessary.
They marched slowly as if [they were] worn out.
Why [are] these tears?
Why [are you] so dejected?
He was ten years of age, his brother [was] eight [years of age].
I have more confidence in James than [I have] in Edmund.
Mary is younger than George [is young].
Tom likes you better than [he likes] me.
You like him better than I do [like him].
I like him better than Charles does [like him].
This racket is not so heavy as that [is heavy].
You are not so old as I [am old].
Peace [be] to his memory!
This is the only pencil [that] I have.

---

[16] *Ellipsis is a Greek word meaning "omission."*

Is that the boy [whom] you hired yesterday?

They say [that] you are going to Europe soon.

[you] Stand up on the bench as I recognised you in the class.

[you] Come here and and help me lifting this load up.

Some examples of Ellipses:

1. Although in a friendly country, they marched always as if in a land of enemies.

2. The aspect of the country was as wild and dreary as the climate.

3. Do not serious and earnest men discuss Hamlet as they would Cromwell or Lincoln?—Lowell.

4. Not so with the others.

5. Though rather shy and distrustful of this new acquaintance, Rip complied with his usual alacrity.

6. Arras was famed for its rich tapestries, Brussels for its carpets, Cambrai for its fine cambric, Lisle for its thread and the fabrics woven from it.

7. Every day brings its task, which, if neglected, is doubled on the morrow.

8. It is not easy to recover an art when once lost.

9. I wish you would go down with me to Newstead.

10. The men are all soldiers, and war and the chase their sole occupation.

11. While in this state of irresolution, she was startled by a low knock.

12. The house was tall, the skylight small and dirty, the day blind with fog, dust and darkness.

13. I little thought you would have deserted me.

14. He is the best Oriental scholar I know.

15. Cromwell was evidently laying, though in an irregular manner, the foundations of an admirable system.

16. He was a foot taller than I.

17. This concerns you rather than me.

18. My father loved Sir Rowland as his soul.

19. This incident points out about you rather than me.

20. She is the best student of our batch I know.

21. Rikin was a mile farther from the destiny than I.

22. We wish You go down to New Town along with us.

Exercise 1

I: Tell whether each of the following sentences is declarative, interrogative, imperative, or exclamatory. If a sentence is both declarative and exclamatory, mention the fact. Mention the subject and the predicate of each sentence. Note all instances of the inverted order.

1. You need not answer this letter. 2. Many surmises of evil alarm the hearts of the people.—Longfellow. 3. Here I am again in the land of old Bunyan. 4. Me this uncharter'd freedom tires.—Wordsworth. 5. Twilight's soft dews steal o'er the village green.—Rogers. 6. Were there many robbers in the band? 7. How will posterity the deed proclaim!—Byron. 8. At dawn the towers of Stirling rang.—Scott. 9. You cannot recall the spoken word.—Emerson. 10. The boughs over my head seemed shadowy with solemn thoughts as well as with rustling leaves.—Hawthorne. 11. So you don't like Raphael! 12. All around lay a frightful wilderness. 13. Why does the sea moan evermore?—Rossetti. 14. What lonely straggler looks along the wave?—Byron. 15. Off went his wig! 16. For some minutes he continued to scrutinize the drawing minutely. 17. Our strength grows out of our weakness.—Emerson. 18. Rudely carved was the porch. 19. What hopes the prince to gain by Lacy's death? 20. Trust thyself. 21. The rest of the men were morose and silent. 22. Here are the ruins of the emperor's palace. 23. Now rumbles along the carriage of some magnate of the city. 24. Wild was the life we led. 25. How poor, and dull, and sleepy, and squalid it seemed! 26. Built are the house and the barn. 27. With what tenderness he sings! 28. Marked ye the younger stranger's eye? 29. One or two idlers, of forbidding aspect, hung about in the murky gaslight. 30. Several mountains crowned with snow shone brilliantly in the distance. 31. Follow me through this passage. 32. Stop me not at your peril. 33. Carry thou this scroll to the castle.

II. Point out the infinitives and the participles. Tell when they occur in verb-phrases. Use them in sentences.

1. I did wrong to smile. 2. Luttrell adjured me with mock pathos to spare his blushes. 3. I begged my friend Sir Roger to go with me into her

hovel. 4. I was wonderfully pleased to see the workings of instinct in a hen followed by a brood of ducks. 5. A man's first care should be to avoid the reproaches of his own heart.—Addison. 6. I was highly entertained to see the gentlemen of the county gathering about my old friend, and striving who should compliment him most. 7. He was let loose among the woods as soon as he was able to ride on horseback. 8. Plutarch says very finely that a man should not allow himself to hate even his enemies. 9. It gives me a serious concern to see such a spirit of dissension in the country.

10. It was his intention to remain there for two or three days. 11. Every part of every carriage had been cleaned, every horse had been groomed. 12. Liberated from the embarrassments of the city, and issuing into the broad uncrowded avenues of the northern suburbs, we soon begin to enter upon our natural pace of ten miles an hour. 13. The beggar, rearing himself against the wall, forgets his lameness. 14. Three miles beyond Barnet, we see approaching another private carriage. 15. We saw many lights moving about as we drew near.

III. Divide each sentence into the complete subject and the complete predicate. If the sentence has a compound subject, mention the substantives that compose it; if the sentence has a compound predicate, mention the verbs (or verb-phrases).

1. The Queen and Prince Albert came to London from Windsor on Saturday morning. 2. You and Lockhart must not abandon the good cause. 3. I saw that he was weak, and took advantage of a pause to remind him not to forget his drive. 4. Two or three of my English biographies have something of the same historical character. 5. Lord Grey, Clanricarde, Labouchere, Vernon Smith, and Seymour will fill up the places. 6. Every change of season, every change of weather, indeed, every hour of the day, produces some change in the magical hues and shapes of these mountains.—Irving. 7. He looked round, and could see nothing but a crow winging its solitary flight across the mountain. 8. They suddenly desisted from their play and stared at him. 9. The sea flashes along the pebbly margin of its silver beach, forming a thousand little bays and inlets, or comes tumbling in among the cliffs of a rock-

bound coast, and beats against its massive barriers with a distant, hollow, continual roar.—Longfellow. 10. A wide gateway ushered the traveller into the interior of the building, and conducted him to a low-roofed apartment, paved with round stones. 11. The strange visitant gruffly saluted me, and, after making several ineffectual efforts to urge his horse in at the door, dismounted and followed me into the room.—Whittier. 12. The foolish and the dead alone never change their opinion.—Lowell. 13. They will slink into their kennels in disgrace, or perchance run wild and strike a league with the wolf and the fox.—Thoreau. 14. Strong will and keen perception overpower old manners and create new.—Emerson. 15. Neither Aristotle, nor Leibnitz, nor Junius, nor Champollion has set down the grammar-rules of this dialect. 16. His mantle and hood were of the best Flanders cloth, and fell in ample and not ungraceful folds. 17. A deep fosse or ditch was drawn round the whole building.

IV. Fill each blank with a single word. Substitute for the word a phrase with the same meaning. Mention in each instance (1) the part of speech, (2) the kind of phrase.

1. He spoke to me ——.
2. The grounds were shut in by a high —— wall.
3. The fire engine —— past.
4. The three girls were laughing ——.
5. The poor child looked —— at the toys.
6. Harold —— the bunch of grapes.
7. The proprietor is a —— man.
8. The archbishop placed upon the king's head a —— crown.
9. The book which I hold in my hand is ——.
10. The —— ordered the Conqueror to open fire.
11. The enemy retreated ——.
12. The rain —— heavily all day.
13. The rain came down —— all day.
14. The —— is in his office.
15. A —— boy came to the door.
16. People know that my brother is president of ——.

Exercise 2

I: Tell whether each sentence is simple, compound, or complex. If the sentence is compound, divide it into its independent clauses, and mention the simple subject (noun or pronoun) and the simple predicate (verb or verb-phrase) of each clause. If the sentence is complex, divide it into the main (independent) and the subordinate clause, and tell whether the latter is used as an adjective or as an adverb.

1. The great gate slowly opened, and a steward and several serving-men appeared. 2. The victors set fire to the wigwams and the fort; the whole was soon in a blaze; many of the old men, the women, and the children perished in the flames. 3. Night closed in, but still no guest arrived. 4. The black waves rolled by them, and the light at the horizon began to fade, and the stars were coming out one by one.—William Black. 5. Mr. Nickleby closed an account book which lay on his desk. 6. By ceaseless action all that is subsists.—Cowper. 7. When the morning broke, the Moorish army had vanished. 8. At midnight, when the town was hushed in sleep, they all went quietly on board. 9. Fortune had cast him into a cavern, and he was groping darkly round. 10. I paced the deserted chambers where he had composed his poem. 11. I strove to speak; my voice utterly failed me. 12. The only avenue by which the town could be easily approached, was protected by a stone wall more than twenty feet high and of great thickness. 13. The night fell tempestuous and wild, and no vestige of the hapless sloop was ever after seen. 14. The simple majesty of this anecdote can gain nothing from any comment which we might make on it. 15. Raleigh speaks the language of the heart of his country when he urges the English statesmen to colonize Guiana.—Froude. 16. Men, in their youth, go to push their fortune in the colony; they succeed; they acquire property there; they return to their native land; they continue to draw the income from their colonial estates.—Brougham. 17. The moonlight glistened upon traces of the gilding which had once covered both rider and steed. 18. While this brief conversation passed, Donatello had once or twice glanced aside with a watchful air. 19. Pray for us, Hilda; we need it.

II. Divide the compound complex sentences into their coördinate clauses. Tell whether each of these clauses, when standing alone, is a simple or a complex sentence.

1. It would be dark before he could reach the village, and he heaved a heavy sigh when he thought of encountering the terrors of Dame Van Winkle. 2. Language gradually varies, and with it fade away the writings of authors who have lived their allotted time. 3. The tallest and handsomest men whom England could produce guarded the passage from the palace gate to the river-side, and all seemed in readiness for the queen's coming forth, although the hour was yet so early. 4. Edward the Confessor died on the fifth of January, 1066, and on the following day an assembly of the thanes and prelates present in London, and of the citizens of the metropolis, declared that Harold should be their king.

III. Point out all the common nouns and all the proper nouns. Mention all the examples of personification.

1. There Guilt his anxious revel kept.—Scott. 2. The first vessel we fell in with was a schooner, which, after a long chase, we made out to be an American. 3. You will be sauntering in St. Peter's perhaps, or standing on the Capitol while the sun sets. 4. I am very deep in my Aristophanes. 5. I saw a most lovely Sir Joshua at Christie's a week ago.—Fitz Gerald. 6. I hear there is scarce a village in England that has not a Moll White in it.—Addison. 7. Such a spirit is Liberty. At times she takes the form of a hateful reptile. She grovels, she hisses, she stings. But woe to those who in disgust shall venture to crush her!—Macaulay. 8. Rough Wulfstane trimmed his shafts and bow.—Scott. 9. To-day we have been a delightful drive through Ettrick Forest, and to the ruins of Newark—the hall of Newark, where the ladies bent their necks of snow to hear "The Lay of the Last Minstrel."—Maria Edgeworth. 10. The same waves wash the moles of the new-built Californian towns, and lave the faded but still gorgeous skirts of Asiatic lands, older than Abraham; while all between float milky-ways of coral isles, and low-lying, endless, unknown Archipelagoes and impenetrable Japans.—Melville. 11. The duchess said haughtily that she had done her best for the Esmonds. 12. To see with one's own eyes men and countries is better than reading all the books of

travel in the world.—Thackeray. 13. Defeat and mortification had only hardened the king's heart. 14. Earth, Ocean, Air, beloved brotherhood!—Shelley. 15. The iron tongue of St. Paul's has told twelve. 16. The Indians, brandishing their weapons, answered only with gestures of angry defiance.

IV. Point out all the abstract, all the collective, and all the compound nouns.

1. The poet binds together by passion and knowledge the vast empire of human society.—Wordsworth. 2. The country is now showing symptoms of greenness and warmth. 3. When the public are gone, we at once put up the great iron shutters. 4. Washington returned to headquarters at Newbury. 5. The Bruce's band moves swiftly on.—Scott. 6. He shall with speed to England.—Shakspere. 7. Soon were dismissed the courtly throng.—Scott. 8. Sickness, desertion, and the loss sustained at Guilford Courthouse had reduced his little army. 9. A detachment was sent against them. 10. Never before this summer have the kingbirds, handsomest of flycatchers, built in my orchard. 11. The young suddenly disperse on your approach, as if a whirlwind had swept them away.—Thoreau. 12. This lighthouse, known to our mariners as Cape Cod or Highland Light, is one of our "primary seacoast lights." 13. We have some salt of our youth in us.—Shakspere. 14. Thou hast nor youth nor age.—Shakspere. 15. The passion for hunting had revived with Washington on returning to his old hunting grounds. 16. A circle there of merry listeners stand.—Byron. 17. The act of the Congress of Vienna remains the eternal monument of their diplomatic knowledge and political sagacity.—Disraeli. 18. Lee undertook the task with alacrity. 19. A row of surfboats and canoes lay along the beach. 20. The situation he had held as aide-de-camp to the commander-in-chief had given him an opportunity of observing the course of affairs. 21. The ground was frozen to a great depth. 22. He was aware of his unpopularity. 23. The stern old war-gods shook their heads.—Emerson.

24. Romanika was the only witness of the incident which took place last night in presence of her fellow friends.

25. We all know that Snehal alone took part in the scheduled event.

26. My name was included in the list of players.

Exercise 3

I: Use am, is, are, was, were, or proper forms as recommended.
1. Oft Music changed, but never ceased her tone.—Byron. 2. Grace Crawley .... at this time living with the two Miss Prettymans.—Trollope. 3. The Catos and the Scipios of the village had gathered in front of the hotel. 4. This gunner .... an excellent mathematician, a good scholar, and a complete sailor.—Defoe. 5. I was, in fact, in the chapel of the Knights Templars.—Irving. 6. The luckless culprit .... brought in, forlorn and chapfallen, in the custody of gamekeepers, huntsmen, and whippers-in, and followed by a rabble rout of country clowns.—Irving. 7. The hare now came still nearer to the place where she .... at first started.—Budgell. 8. The Fairfaxes .... no longer at hand.—Irving. 9. All the peers and peeresses put on their coronets. 10. Time .... no longer slow; his sickle mows quickly in this age.—Disraeli. 11. Under the humblest roof, the commonest person in plain clothes .... (sit) there massive, cheerful, yet formidable, like the Egyptian colossi.—Emerson. 12. Within forty-eight hours, hundreds of horse and foot .... (come) by various roads to the city. 13. The hart and hind .... (wander) in a wilderness abounding in ferny coverts and green and stately trees.—Disraeli. 14. The ship had received a great deal of damage, and it required some time to repair her.—Defoe. 15. When Mary, the nurse, returns with the little Miss Smiths from Master Brown's birthday party, she .... narrowly questioned as to their behavior. 16. Of all our fleet, consisting of a hundred and fifty sail, scarce twelve appeared.—Smollett. 17. Hindoos, Russians, Chinese, Spaniards, Portuguese, Englishmen, Frenchmen, Genoese, Neapolitans, Venetians, Greeks, Turks, descendants from all the builders of Babel, ... (come) to trade at Marseilles, sought the shade alike.—Dickens. 18. There lies the port; the vessel puffs her sail.—Tennyson. 19. I .... (has/ have/had) desire to see the old family seat of the Lucys.—Irving. 20. The Miss Lambs .... the belles of little Britain.—Irving. 21. Lord Culloden at length appeared with his daughters, Ladies Flora and Grizell.—Disraeli. 22. Still his honied wealth Hymettus yields.—Byron. 23. Josephine .... (has/ have/ had) been made executrix of her father's estate. 24. Georgette crouched by the fire, reading a wonderful

tale of kings, princesses, enchanted castles, knights and ladies, monks and nuns, wizards and witches. 25. She .... a vixen when she .... (go) to school.—Shakspere. 26. Keep a gamester from the dice and a good student from his book.—Shakspere. 27. They .... sheep and calves which seek out assurance in that.— Shakspere. 28. A score of good ewes .... (may/ might) be worth ten pounds.—Shakspere. 29. Let ay's seem no's and no's seem ay's.—Gay.

II. Mention all the nouns that are in the nominative case, and give the construction (or syntax) of each,—as subject, predicate nominative, vocative (or nominative of direct address), exclamatory nominative, or nominative in apposition.

1. A weary lot is thine, fair maid.—Scott. 2. At last, our small acquaintance, Ned Higgins, trudged up the street, on his way to school.—Hawthorne. 3. The soil is in general a moist and retentive clay. 4. Rumors alone were their guides through a wild and desolate country.—Longfellow. 5. Young man, have you challenged Charles the wrestler?—Shakspere. 6. Ralph was an Eton boy, and hence, being robust and shrewd, a swimmer and a cricketer. 7. Here Harold was received a welcome guest.—Scott. 8. The tall Highlander remained obdurate. 9. The beams and rafters, roughly hewn and with strips of bark still on them, and the rude masonry of the chimneys, made the garret look wild and uncivilized. 10. Deathlike the silence seemed. 11. Sorrow and silence are strong, and patient endurance is godlike.—Longfellow. 12. Fly, fly, detested thoughts, forever from my view!—Beattie. 13. Time must not be counted by calendars, but by sensation, by thought.— Disraeli. 14. This is the history of Charlotte Corday. 15. The nabobs soon became a most unpopular class of men. 16. Before him stretched the long, laborious road, dry, empty, and white.—Hardy. 17. With the great mass of mankind, the test of integrity in a public man is consistency.— Macaulay. 18. These are trifles, Mr. Premium. 19. My thanks are due to you for your trouble and care. 20. Here's my great uncle, Sir Richard Ravelin. 21. Rowley, my old friend, I am sure you congratulate me. 22. David, you are a coward! 23. Here come other Pyncheons, the whole tribe, in their half-a-dozen generations. 24. Uncle Venner, trundling a wheelbarrow, was the earliest person stirring in the neighborhood. 25. Up the chimney roared the fire, and brightened the room with its broad

blaze. 26. Liberty! freedom! tyranny is dead!—Shakspere. 27. The hostess's daughter, a plump Flanders lass, with long gold pendants in her ears, was at a side window.—Irving. 28. Horses! can these be horses that bound off with the action and gesture of leopards?—De Quincey. 29. Peace! silence! Brutus speaks. 30. The rains, frosts, and tempests splinter the chalk above and the waves gnaw it away below.—Geikie.

III. Parse nouns in the following.

1. Such was the narrative of Jack Grant, the mate. 2. Rippling waters made a pleasant moan.—Byron. 3. Swiftly they hurried away to the forge of Basil the blacksmith.—Longfellow. 4. A pale fog hung over London. 5. So like a shattered column lay the king.—Tennyson. 6. Then sing, ye birds, sing, sing a joyous song.—Wordsworth. 7. A blighted spring makes a barren year.—Johnson. 8. Dark and neglected locks overshadowed his brow. 9. Imagine the wind howling, the sea roaring, the rain beating. 10. Lay these vain regrets aside. 11. Birds of passage sailed through the leaden air. 12. Authority forgets a dying king.— Tennyson. 13. Three years she grew in sun and shower.—Wordsworth. 14. The sound of horns came floating from the valley, prolonged by the mountain echoes. 15. Hours had passed away like minutes. 16. Your mistrust cannot make me a traitor.—Shakspere. 17. She halted a moment before speaking. 18. The room opened on a terrace adorned with statues and orange trees. 19. The sun is coming down to earth, and the fields and the waters shout to him golden shouts.—Meredith. 20. England is unrivalled for two things—sports and politics.—Disraeli. 21. Thus we lived several years in a state of much happiness. 22. The old gentleman's whole countenance beamed with a serene look of indwelling delight. 23. I am reading Selwyn's "Correspondence," a remarkable book. 24. I have lived my life.—Tennyson. 25. My heart is like a singing bird.—Christina Rossetti. 26. How like a winter hath my absence been.—Shakspere. 27. Three weeks we westward bore.—Longfellow. 28. It rains pitchforks.— Fitz Gerald. 29. The sublimer and more passionate poets I still read, by snatches and occasionally.—De Quincey. 30. Coningsby slept the deep sleep of youth and health.—Disraeli.

31. Thou mightst call him a goodly person. 32. My father named me Autolycus. 33. A country fellow brought him a huge fish.

Exercise 4

I: Use am, is, are, was ,were, shall, will, has, have, had, or proper form of verbs:

1. Pennon and banner wave no more. 2. They soon …….. (gain) the utmost verge of the forest, and entered the country inhabited by men without vice.—Goldsmith. 3. Our avenue ……………… strewn with the whole crop of autumn's withered leaves.—Hawthorne. 4. He ……………… the rich man who can avail himself of all men's faculties.—Emerson. 5. Like an awakened conscience, the sea ……………… moaning and tossing.—Longfellow. 6. He again ……….. (call) and whistled after his dog. 7. She ………..(write) and addressed a hurried note. 8. The light and warmth of that long-vanished day ………. (live) with me still. 9. Violet and primrose girls, and organ boys with military monkeys, and systematic bands very determined in tone if not in tune, ……………. (fill) the atmosphere.—Meredith. 10. The blood ……….. (leave) Wilfrid's ashen cheek. 11. …………. (give) us manners, virtue, freedom, power!—Wordsworth. 12. A great deal of shrubbery ……….. (cluster) along the base of the stone wall, and takes away the hardness of its outline. 13. I ………….. (travel) the whole four hundred miles between this and Madras on men's shoulders. 14. Here we ………. (set up) twelve little huts like soldiers' tents. 15. Swiftly they ……… (glide) away, like the shade of a cloud on the prairie. 16. Athens, even long after the decline of the Roman empire, still …………. (continue) the seat of ………. (learn), politeness, and wisdom.—Goldsmith. 17. Four times the sun ……………… risen and set. 18. Speak! speak! ……… fearful guest! 19. The oak …………. (rise) before me like a pillar of darkness. 20. Another long blast …………. (fill) the old courts of the castle with its echoes, and ……………… answered by the warder from the walls. 21. Sound, sound the clarion, fill the fife!—Scott. 22. Now, Falstaff, where ……………… you been all this while? 23. Sounds of a horn they heard, and the distant lowing of cattle. 24. Homer ……………… always his companion now. 25. Forgive me these injurious suspicions. 26. O, pride! pride! it …………. (deceive) me with the subtlety of a serpent. 27. I ……….. (make) Mr. Wright's gardener a present of fifty sorts of plant seeds. 28. Your mother and I last week …………. (make) a trip to Gayhurst, the seat of Mr. Wright, about four miles off.

Exercise 5

I: Parse Persona Pronouns in the following.

1. She peeped from the window into the garden. 2. The little marquis immediately threw himself into the attitude of a man about to tell a long story. 3. It pours and it thunders, it lightens amain.—Scott. 4. Master, master, look about you! 5. Leontine, with his own and his wife's fortune, bought a farm of three hundred a year.—Addison. 6. The Tories carry it among the new members six to one.—Swift. 7. I wrote to him, but could tell him nothing. 8. On the next morning after breakfast the major went out for a walk by himself. 9. Their hearts quaked within them, at the idea of taking one step farther. 10. Mrs. Forrester's surprise was equal to ours. 11. It's twenty years since he went away from home. 12. I seated myself in a recess of a large bow window. 13. At the last moment his heart failed him, and he looked round him for some mode of escape. 14. A friend of mine has been spending some time at Sir Walter Scott's.

15. Send me a letter directed to me at Mr. Watcham's. 16. I have lately received from my bookseller a copy of my subscribers' names. 17. We came in our first morning's march to very good springs of fresh water. 18. We are both of us inclined to be a little too positive. 19. Heyne's best teacher was himself.—Carlyle.

20. Aspasia, you have lived but few years in the world, and with only one philosopher—yourself. 21. I got to the side in time to see a huge liner's dim shape slide by like a street at night; she would have been invisible but for her row of lights. 22. The cataracts blow their trumpets from the steep.—Wordsworth. 23. I am he they call Old Care.—Peacock. 24. The sharp and peevish tinkle of the shop-bell made itself audible. 25. The heroes themselves say, as often as not, that fame is their object. 26. He seems to himself to touch things with muffled hands. 27. She took counsel with herself what must be done. 28. The head of the Pyncheons found himself involved in serious financial difficulties. 29. Ha! here is Hepzibah herself!

***

5. Active and Passive Voice

<u>Rules for conversion from Active to Passive Voice</u>

1. The subject and object are interchanged
2. The preposition BY is added before the object
3. The verb is changed to past participle (3rd form of verb)
4. A new auxiliary is added to the Past Participle form of verb.
5. If the subject or the object in an active voice sentence is a pronoun (I, we, you, he, she, they, it) it changes: (I-me; we-us; you-you; he-him; she-her; they-them; it-it) and vice-versa. e.g. I wrote a letter – A letter was written by me. The prefect does keep accusing me daily – I am being accused by the prefect daily.
6. If the subject in the active voice sentence is unknown or unimportant or obvious, by + object is omitted. We make butter from cow's milk. Butter is made from cow's milk.
7. If the verb in the active voice sentence has a modal in it, the verb is changed to – modal + be + the past participle. e.g. Rajesh can lift this box. This box can be lifted by Rajesh. We should obey the rules. The rules should be obeyed.
8. When there are two objects, only one object is interchanged. The second object remains unchanged. (He told me a story – He-subject; me – object 1; a story – object 2) (I was told a story by him; A story was told to me by him)

The table below shows how the verb is changed into its passive voice form in different tenses.

Tense	Active Voice	Passive Voice
The simple present	He eats an apple	An apple is eaten by him.
The present continuous	He is eating an apple.	An apple is being eaten by him.
The present perfect	He has eaten an apple.	An apple has been eaten by him.
The simple past	He ate an apple.	An apple was eaten by him.
The past continuous	He was eating an apple	An apple was being eaten by him
The past perfect	He had eaten an apple	An apple had been eaten by him
The simple future	He will eat an apple	An apple will be eaten by him.
The Future continuous	He will be eating an apple.	An apple will have been eaten by him.
The Future in the past	He would have eaten an apple	An apple would have been eaten by him

Note: Some of the sentences like – sentences constructed using auxiliary verbs(Hariharan is a good boy); perfect continuous tenses (in all the three time periods – Present, Past, Future) (My room mate has been copying my homework) and intransitive verbs (I go to temple or she has gone to the market) cannot be converted into passive form . When the verb in a sentence shows that the subject is not the doer of the action, the verb is in the passive voice. (Generally you will find "by" in the sentence. If "by" is not there, you can put a question "Who?", you will get an answer.) When the verb in a sentence shows that the subject is the doer of the action, the verb is in the active voice.

Exercise 1

Q 1. Choose the best way of continuing after each sentence.

1. He lives in a small house. a) Somebody built it about forty years ago.
      b) It was built about forty years ago.
2. English is worth learning. a) People speak it in a lot of countries.
      b) It is spoken in a lot of countries.
3. He got a sport car, but he didn't like it. a) So he sold it again.
      b) So it was sold again.
4. My nephew is an artist. a) He has just painted another picture.
      b) Another picture has just been painted by him.
5. The new Virginia Meyer film is marvellous.
   a) They are showing it at our local cinema.
   b) It is being shown at our local cinema.

Q 2. Choose the best sentence from each pair to build up a continuous text.

   E.g.: a) *How books are made?*
         b) *How people make books?*
1.   a) First of all, printers print big sheets of papers.
      b) First of all, big sheets of papers are printed.
2.   a) Each sheet contains the text of a number of pages (e.g. 32).
      b) Each text of a number of pages (e.g. 32) is contained in each sheet.
3.   a) People fold and cut the sheets to produce sections of the book.
      b) The sheets are folded and cut to produce sections of the book.
4.   a) These sections are called signatures.
      b) We call these sections signatures.
5.   a) The printers put all the signatures together in a correct order.
      b) All the signatures are put together in a correct order.
6.   a) Then they are bound together and their edges are trimmed.
      b) Then they bind the signatures together and trim the edges.
7.   a) Finally, the cover — which has been printed separately — is attached.
      b) Finally, they attach the cover — which they have printed separately.
8.   a) Now the publishers can publish the book.
      b) Now the book can be published.

Q 3.

A) Rewrite these instructions, using simple commands instead of the passive.

A regular size sheet of typing paper (8½ x 11 inches of A4) needs to be used for this experiment. First of all, it has to be torn into four smaller pieces. This is done as follows:

1. It has to be folded in the middle and then it can be torn into two pieces.

2. Each piece is folded again across the middle and torn to make a total of four equal-size pieces.

Now one of the pieces is placed on the table with the long sides pointing down. A horizontal line is drawn across the top of the paper about a quarter of the way from the top. Then two vertical lines are drawn downwards from the horizontal line, so that the bottom part of the paper is divided into three equal-size parts.

Next, the paper has to be torn along each of these vertical lines as far as the horizontal line so that three flaps are created. Then the left flap is folded towards you and the right flap is folded away from you — the folds are made right at the top of the flap. The centre flap should not be not folded, though.

Now a paper clip has to be found and this is attached to the bottom of the centre flap. Finally, the whole thing has to be raised high and is then allowed to fall…

Begin like this:

Use a regular-size sheet of a typing paper (8½ x 11 inches of A4) for this experiment. First of all, tear it into four smaller pieces. Do this as follows: ...

B) Carry out the experiment, following the instructions you have written.

Q 4. Rewrite these newspaper headlines as complete sentences, using the passive.

E.g.: Theft of valuable painting from National Gallery.
    A valuable painting has been stolen from the National Gallery.

1. Over 100 highway deaths last month

2. Over 24,000 new businesses begun last year

3. Spacecraft discovers new planet beyond Pluto

4. 15 students arrested after demonstration

5. Mexico wins soccer championship

6. Manager accused of the accepting bribes — forced to resign

7. Missing airliner found in jungle — survivors rescued by helicopter

1. Rewrite these sentences in the passive, using appropriate tense or modal:
1. They destroyed the original picture years ago.
2. They have never explained the events of that night.
3. You shouldn't store cleaning fluid and soft drinks together.
4. You can buy film for this camera anywhere.
5. They took the stolen goods across the frontier.
6. You will show passes when entering the building.
7. They had told her to make an application.

2. Complete these sentences using a passive construction. Only use* by *if it's natural to do so.
1. A bus nearly hit Keith while he was trying to cross the road. *(Keith...)*
2. Luckily lightning doesn't strike many people.
3. The incident shouldn't harm relations between the police and the community.
4. The snow is very heavy. British Rail has cancelled all trains to Scotland.
5. The police officer is interviewing her about the crime.
6. The burglars have stolen my stereo and television.

3. Change the passive sentences in the letter into the active.
Dear Madame,

It is with regret that we now give the formal notice that your account has been closed. Your credit limit has been exceeded by over $ 200. Customers are asked to apply in writing if they wish their credit to be extended, and this was not done. You were warned last month that this would be the result. In accordance with the conditions of use, a copy of which has already been sent to you, the whole of the balance is payable with immediate effect.

You are required to return to us your credit card, but before doing so it should be cut in half for security.

A pre-addressed envelope (not pre-paid) is enclosed.

Yours faithfully,

R. J. Box,

General Manager

4. Turn these newspapers headlines into radio news headlines. (Informal, spoken form.)
*   "Highjacked jet blown up"

- "Cure for cancer at last"
- "7 pickets arrested in miners' strike"
- "40 killed in train crash in Sweden"

5. Complete each sentence using a passive construction.
1. — I'm glad that horrible man (catch).
   — Yes, I'm sure he (send) to prison.
2. — When I saw him he (question) by the police.
   — I think he (give) a very long sentence.
3. — The postman told me he (bite) by a dog.
   — (Take) to hospital?
4. — I hear that a lot of Irish jokes (include) in tonight's show.
   — Oh, no! I hate it when insulting jokes (tell) about other nationalities.

6. Choose the best form.
On Tuesday August 11th 1911 a young artist, Louis Beraud, (1) at the Louvre in Paris to complete a painting of the Salon Carre. This was the room where the world's famous paintings, the Mona Lisa by Leonardo da Vinci, was on display. To his surprise, there was an empty space where the painting (2). A guard told him it probably (3). An hour later several visitors had complained about the missing picture, and so the guard went enquire about it. At eleven o'clock the museum authorities realised that the painting (4). The police (5), but it was 3 p.m. before the exits (6). The newspapers (7) at 4 p.m., and the next day headlines all over the world announced the theft.
Actually the Leonardo (8) for more than 24 hours before anyone noticed it was missing.

1.A)has arrived
   B)arrived
   C)had been arrived

2.A)should be
   B)is
   C)should have been

3.A)being photographed
   B)was being photographed
   C)was photographed

4.A)had been stolen
   B)was stolen
   C)had stolen

5.A)had been called
   B)were called
   C)was called

6.A)were locked
   B)locked
   C)had been locked

7.A)have been told
   B)has been told
   C)were told

8.A)had gone
   B)had been gone
   C)was gone

Q 5. Practice saying these sentences and answer the questions.

1. a) The secretary will mail these letters to morrow. b) These letters will be mailed tomorrow, and what about these ones?
2. a) Someone ought to wash those dishes right away. b) Those dishes ought to be washed right away, and what about these ones?
3. a) The factory produced 5,000 cars every day last year. b) 5,000 cars were produced every day last year, and what about this year?
4. a) People drink a great deal of tea in England. b) A great deal of tea is drunk in England, and what about your country?
5. a) Craftsmen make many beautiful objects of paper in Japan. b) Many beautiful objects of paper are made in Japan, and what about India?
6. a) They used to sell medicine here. b) Medicine is used to be sold here, and where is it sold now?
7. a) You must return these books within a fortnight. b) These books must be returned within a fortnight, and what about those ones?
8. a) A gang of workmen built this house in 1840. b) This house was built in 1840, and what about this one?

Q 6. Change these sentences as in the example. Then think about why this mistakes them better, and check your answers in the key.

E.g.: That she had not written to her parents for over two years surprised me. *I was surprised that she had not written to her parents for over two years.*
1. That nobody was prepared to take him to hospital shocked us.
2. That Mary wanted to tell everybody what to do annoyed me.
3. That George rang me up at three o'clock in the morning to tell me he was in love again didn't please me.
4. That the sailor reported us about advancing storm while we were preparing to sail for fishing early in the morning.
5. That nobody expected Rikin as a winner of the challenging cup.
6. That she wanted to move upstairs for finishing her make ups.
7. That she was too early taking her stand to go to the opposition bench.
8. That her motive regarding visit to the park changed dramatically, we also changed our plan.
9. That Snehal visited my home early in the morning to tell me about her plan of visiting countryside along with some of her friends.
10. That Rohan approached me to let me know about his success in sports meet for which he had prepared a lot.

Exercise 2

Q 1. Put the sentences into the Passive Voice where possible.

1. Goldfish live in fresh water.
2. The Egyptians built pyramids.
3. Walked 4 miles yesterday.
4. They arrived at 7 last night.
5. They informed me about it.
6. I slept till 8.
7. It's raining.
8. You must obey the rules.
9. He's sneezing again.
10. You can buy videos like this anywhere.
11. Someone has to write the history of this place.
12. The have sold their car to pay the debts.
13. They hold a meeting in the village hall once a week.
14. They have proved that there is no life in the Moon.
15. They owe a lot of money to Moscow Narodny Bank.

Q 2. Rewrite the sentences, putting the underlined verbs into the Passive. Make any other changes where necessary.

1. They should <u>have given</u> us this information ages ago. *This information should have been given to us ages ago.*
2. Do you want to someone to <u>wake you up</u> in the morning?
3. I don't like someone <u>telling</u> me what to do.
4. The windows are really dirty: no-one<u>'s cleaned</u> them for weeks.
5. After the company <u>made</u> him redundant, he became very depressed.
6. I would like them to <u>have given</u> me the chance to explain my point of view, but they weren't interested.
7. I'm hoping they <u>will choose</u> me for the college football team.
8. People <u>believe</u> that many more people will die of skin cancer over the next ten years.
9. If it hadn't rained so much, we would <u>have finished</u> the job on time.
10. We can't take the car: the people at the garage <u>are repairing</u> it.

Q 3. Most of the sentences contain one mistake. Correct it of write "right".

1. My neighbour is very proud of her new grandson Kiriusha who born last week.

2. I'm very fond of this old brooch because it was belonged to my grandmother.
3. My family live in Montego Bay but I was educated in Kingston.
4. I'm afraid I can't lend you my camera. It's repairing this week.
5. The bridge was collapsed during the floods but fortunately no one was using it at the time.
6. If you aren't careful what you're doing with that hammer someone will hurt in a minute!
7. The word "stupid" was in my report but it wasn't referred to you.
8. I'm sorry I'm late. I got held up in the traffic.
9. When did you discover that the money had been disappeared?
10. Children under the age of seven do not allow in this pool.

Q 4. Put in the correct forms, active or passive, of the verbs in brackets.
HOW THE OTHER HALF LIVES

Lord Manning was a rich and famous banker. When he (die), he (give) a magnificent funeral which (attend) by hundreds of famous people. The funeral was going to (hold) in Westminster Abbey. Many ordinary people (line) the streets to watch the procession. The wonderful black and gold carriage (draw) by 16 black horses. The mourners (follow) in silence. Lord Mannings (give) a royal farewell. Two tramps were among the crowd , they (watch) the procession. As solemn music (can/hear) in the distance, one of them (turn) to the other and (whisper) in admiration: "Now, that's what I call really living!"

Q 5. Put in the correct forms, active or passive, of the verbs in brackets.
FISHY TALES

Mermaids (see) … by sailors for centuries. The basis of all mermaids myths (suppose) …to be a creature called a Manatee: a kind of walrus! Mermaids used to (show) …in funfairs until recently. It all began in 1817 when a "mermaid" (buy) …for $6,00 by a sailor in South Pacific. She (eventually sell) …to the great circus owner Barnum. She (exhibit) …in 1842 as "The Feejee Mermaid". It (say)… that she earned Barnum $ 1,000 a week! The thousands who saw this mermaid (must/disappoint)… . She (cleverly make) …by a Japanese fisherman. A monkey's head (delicately sew) …to the tail of a large salmon. The job (so skilfully do) …that the joint between the fish and the monkey was invisible. Real imagination (must/require) …to see this revolting creature as a beautiful mermaid combing her golden hair!

Q 6. Use passive or active, in any appropriate tense, for the verbs in brackets.

1. The Amazon valley is extremely important to the ecology of the earth. Forty percent of the world's oxygen (produce) there.
2. The game (win, probably) by the other team tomorrow. They're a lot better than we are.
3. There was a terrible accident on a busy downtown street yesterday. Dozens of people (see) it, including my friend, who (interview) by the police.
4. In my country, certain prices (control) by the government, such as prices for medical supplies. However, other prices (determine) by how much people are willing to pay for a product.
5. Yesterday the wind (blow) my hat off my head. I had to chase it down the street. I (want, not) to lose it because it's my favourite hat and it (cost) me a lot.
6. Right now Alex is in the hospital. He (treat) for a bad burn on his hand and arm.
7. Yesterday a purse-snatcher (catch) by a dog. While the thief (chase) by the police, he (jump) over a fence into someone's yard, where he encountered a ferocious dog. The dog (keep) the thief from escaping.
8. Frostbite may occur when the skin (expose) to extreme cold. It most frequently (affect) the skin of the cheeks, chin, ears, fingers, nose, and toes.
9. The first fish (appear) on the earth about 500 million years ago. Up to now, over 20,000 kinds of fish (name) and (describe) by scientists. New species (discover) every day, so the total increases continually.
10. Proper first aid can save a victim's life, especially if the victim is bleeding heavily, has stopped breathing, of (poison).
11. The government used to support the school. Today it (support) by private funds as well as by the tuition the students pay.
12. Richard Anderson is a former astronaut. Several years ago, at the age of 52, Anderson (inform) by his superior at the aircraft corporation that he could no longer be a test pilot. He (tell) that he was being relieved from his duties because of his age. Claiming age discrimination, he took the corporation to court.
13. In the early 80's, photographs of Mars (send) back to earth by unmanned space probes. From these photographs, scientists have been able to make detailed maps of the surface of Mars.
14. A network of lines (discover) on Mars' surface by an Italian astronomer around the turn of the century. The astronomer (call) these lines" channels", but when the Italian word (translate) into English, it became "canals". As a result, some people thought the

lines were waterways that (build) by some unknown living creatures. We know that the lines are not really canals. Canals (exist, not) on Mars.

Q 7. *Supply the required passive forms of the verbs in brackets.*

1. Aunt Dinah (not to like) by my father's family; she (to consider) vulgar.
2. After his brother's departure Paul sat for a long time thinking about what (to say).
3. "I'm not prepared", my father said, "to listen to your suggestions that you never (to treat) fairly at school".
4. In the drawing-room the music of Mozart (to play) by an orchestra seen on the screen.
5. "Remember I (to pay) by an hour"' grumbled the driver.
6. But there were signs that order (to restore) in the town.
7. I (to receive) by one of the chiefs and (to take) for lunch to the canteen.
8. Well, what (to do) about it, Ted?
9. He went into the bedroom. The bed (to turn) down for the night by a naked maid many hours before.
10. Please find out of our father (to see) to leave.
11. She could have gone to Cambridge if she had wanted, she (to offer) a scholarship.
12. He arrived just after the electricity (to cut), and Joseph was lighting the oil-lamps.
13. On Friday she (to give) two weeks' notice at the Works.
14. Then the voice announced that the passengers (to ask) to pass through the Customs.
15. I wondered to what extent she (to influence) by his name to accept the offer.
16. Meg (to look) upon as a perfect wife for a terrorist.
17. Such are the matters that (to deal) with in Mr. Burrough's book.
18. He (see) entering the school building just when the first student (call) upon to read aloud from the Beowulf.
19. Ahead of us the port lay in a flood of lights. Two cargo-ships (to unload) a shipment of cocaine.
20. I found the idea of going to Hereford very upsetting because I (to promise) a very nice job a couple of weeks before.
21. Not far away she noticed the film manager in whose office she once (to make) to feel so ridiculous.
22. "You must be very prosperous, Jimmy, to own a car like that." "This car (to lend) to me by an American woman."

Exercise 3

Q 1. Rewrite the sentences, putting the underlined verbs into the Passive. Make any other changes necessary. Reproduce the dialogues in the Reported Speech.

Jane is talking to her friend Greg about her holiday.

G: So, how was the holiday?

J: Oh, it was fantastic. They <u>organised</u> everything so well. As soon as we arrived at the airport, our courier <u>met</u> us and <u>took</u> us to hotel. Someone <u>had cleaned</u> all the rooms beautifully and <u>put</u> fresh flowers on the tables.

G: Oh, how lovely. And what about the food?

J: It was excellent. They freshly <u>prepared</u> it all in the hotel and they even <u>made</u> the bread in the hotel kitchen. They <u>served</u> bread rolls hot every morning with breakfast.

G: Mm, it does sound good. I must say, I'd like someone <u>to cook</u> my meals for me for a couple of weeks. And what about the surrounding area? Was that nice?

J: Oh, beautiful. There were trips every day and they <u>showed</u> us all the local sights. There was so much history to see, You'd love it there, honestly.

Q 2. Read this information about what happened to the Watsons.

Someone broke into the Watsons' house at the weekend. The burglar took some jewellery. But he didn't do any damage. A young policewoman interviewed Mrs Watson. The police found some fingertips, and the police computer identified the burglar. The police have arrested a man and are questioning him.

Complete the passive sentences in this conversation. Use phrase with **by** only if it adds information.

Mrs Watson: *Our house was broken into at the weekend.*

Mrs Owen: Oh, no!

Mrs Watson: Some jewellery __(1)__ . But no damage __(2)__ .

Mrs Owen: Did the police come and see you?

Mrs Watson: Yes, of course. I __(3)__ .

Mrs Owen: Do they know who the burglar was?

Mrs Watson: Oh, yes. Some __(4)__ , and the __(5)__ . A man __(6)__ .

Mrs Owen: Oh, good. Well, I hope you get your jewellery back.

Q 3. Rewrite the sentences beginning in the way shown. Do not use __by__ unless it is important to the meaning.

1. The company has cut all salaries.
   All salaries *have been cut.*

2. The bank manager kept me waiting for half an hour.
   I ____

3. Employers must pay all travel expenses for this training course.
   All   travel   expenses   for   this   training   course
   ____

4. Do you suppose your brother could have written such a letter?
   Do you suppose such a letter ______________________________

5. They use a computer to do that job nowadays.
   A computer ____

6. During the recession, the firm was making people redundant almost every week.
   During the recession people ______________________________

7. Nobody informed the police that there had been a mistake.
   The police ____

8. Where will your company send you next year?
   Where will you ____?

9. The news about the famine distressed Josephine.
   Josephine ____

10. I've still got the camera because no none has claimed it.
    I've still got the camera because it _____________________

11. Has anyone ever asked you for your opinion?
    Have you ____?

Some verbs can have two objects – an indirect object (the person receiving something) and a direct object (the thing that someone gives)

	Direct	Indirect
Kate gave	*me*	*this cassette.*
I'll send	*my cousin*	*a present.*

We can say the same thing with a different pattern.

	Direct	Indirect for
Kate gave	*the cassette*	*to someone else.*
I'll send	*a present*	*to my cousin.*

a) We can use the *to* pattern or an indirect object with the verbs of giving: **give, lend, hand, pass, throw; send, post, bring, take; pay, sell; promise; show, offer; read, write, tell, teach; owe; leave (in a will).**

In an active sentence, a verb of giving can have two different patterns after it. They both have the same meaning.

> *The Queen gave **a medal to the pilot.***
> *The Queen gave **the pilot a medal.***

Verbs with two objects have two possible passive structures. Either a medal or the pilot can be the subject of a passive sentence:

A medal *was given to the pilot.*
The pilot *was given a medal.*

The first of these two sentences is about a medal, and it tells us who received it. The second is about the pilot, and it tells us what he received. We choose the structure which fits best with what comes before and after. The structure with the **person** as subject is probably more common.

ACTIVE PASSIVE

*They gave **the winner a prize**.*   ***The winner was given** a prize.*

*They gave **a prize to the winner**.*   ***A prize was given** to the winner.*

Q 4. Change the structure

1. Nothing was sent to me. *I was sent nothing.*
2. Papers were brought to us to sign.
3. A clock was given to Henry when he retired.
4. Stories were read to the children.
5. ‡ 5,000 is owed to me.
6. A new job has been offered to me.
7. A car has been lent to me for the week.
8. A full explanation was promised to us.
9. A lot of lies were told to me by the secretary.
10. Useful work skills are taught to our staff.
11. Company shares are offered to most employees.
12. People with initiative are given opportunities.
13. Six weeks' holiday is allowed to all employees.
14. People moving house are given help.
15. Women who leave to have children are paid a sum of money.

b) We can use the **for** pattern or an indirect object with these verbs: **buy, get, fetch, bring; find; leave, save; reserve, order, book; make, cook, build; pick, choose:**

They found a spare ticket for me. OR *They found me a spare ticket.*

With these verbs practically only one passive construction is used, i. e. When the direct object becomes the subject of the Passive Construction: A spare ticket was found for me.

Q 5. Change the structure using the Passive Voice (give two variants where possible).

1. Tim lent Sarah his calculator.
2. Brian sent a message to his wife.
3. I sold my bike to my brother.
4. The boss promised the workers a pay rise.
5. I've saved you a seat.
6. Someone passed the sugar to Dave.
7. Peter told the joke to all his friends.
8. Sam gave his flat-mate some help.
9. I am making our guests a cake.
10. Could you send me a bill?
11. I have bought a present for you.
12. My brother read the letter to me.
13. He is showing Granny his picture.
14. Tom fetched some books to Monica.
15. We owe $ 20,000 to the bank.
16. He will get some beer to me.
17. I wrote my teacher a letter of apology.
18. Sarah threw the ball to Kirsty.
19. They showed her the shortest way to the station.
20. My mother taught me English.
21. Tom has just told me a good story.
22. She will lend me this book on Tuesday.
23. My friend gave me a good piece of advice how to do this job.
24. She told us her name after we had asked her twice.
25. I sent her brother a telegram.
26. Jill had paid the money to the cashier before the shop was closed.

c) The verbs: **explain, describe, dictate, repeat, mention, say, suggest, introduce, declare, deliver, present, recommend, prove, point out** do not have the indirect object first. With these verbs only one Passive Construction is used.

Q 6. *Change the structure using the Passive Voice.*

1. Can you explain the plan to us?
2. I've come to say goodbye to you.
3. I suggested a new method to her.
4. Describe your wife to me.
5. The teacher is dictating new words to the students.
6. He won't repeat his orders to them.
7. His brother has already mentioned this interesting detail to me.
8. The court declared to us that the bank was bankrupt.
9. The host had introduced all his guests to his cousin before the meals were brought.
10. Who delivers the mail to you?
11. The expert will prove this fact to you at the next meeting.
12. The lecturer has pointed out this interesting detail to the audience.
13. She decided to devote her life to handicapped people.

"I have been explaining this rule to you for two hours," – he said irritably.

Q 7. *Rewrite the sentences, putting the underlined verbs into the Passive. Make any other changes necessary.*

The company is sorry to announce that the situation has forced it to introduce a range of cost-cutting measures as from the beginning of the new year. Unfortunately, we can no longer provide free tea and coffee. Someone is going to install new coin-operated machines in every department and you can purchase a wide range of drinks from these. We will also stop overtime payments after the end of this month and we will expect all members of staff to complete their duties within their contact hours. You must no longer make personal calls from office phones and we request you to use the payphone in the basement for this purpose.

Exercise 4

Q 1. *Create sentences with get and the given words.*

Confused	dressed	bored
married	finished	elected
done	lost	worried
excited	hurt	prepared
scared	cheated	wrinkled

In a passive sentences we mentioned the agent, the person or thing doing action, only if it is important. We do not mention the agent when:

1.   the agent does not add any new information:

The money was stolen.

The men were arrested last night.

We do not need to say that the money was stolen **by a thief** or that the men were arrested **by the police.**

2.   the agent is not important:

The streets are cleaned every day.

Oil has been discovered in Bavaria.

Who discovered the oil is less important than the fact that it is there.

3.   it is difficult to say who the agent is:

This kind of jacket is considered very smart.

> *A number of attempts have been made to the Loch Ness*
> *monster.*

Empty subject (**you, they, people** etc.)

We can use an 'empty subject' such as you, one, they, people or someone. We can sometimes use them instead of the passive, especially in conversation. Compare:

<table>
<tr><td>ACTIVE</td><td>PASSIVE</td></tr>
<tr><td>*You/One should check the details.*</td><td>*The details should be checked.*</td></tr>
<tr><td>*They're increasing the rents.*</td><td>*The rents are being increased.*</td></tr>
<tr><td>*People use this footpath every day.*</td><td>*This footpath is used every day.*</td></tr>
<tr><td>*Someone took my purse.*</td><td>*My purse was taken.*</td></tr>
</table>

Q 2. Rewrite these verbs as passives, keeping them in the same tense, and removing <u>they, we, someone,</u> *etc.*

1. We clean the garages every day.
   The garages are cleaned every day.

2. Someone has given him a lot of money.
3. The police arrested two hundred people.
4. We check every car engine thoroughly.
5. We export this computer to seventy different countries.
6. They have cancelled the meeting.
7. We opened the factory at nine o'clock.
8. They send two million books to America every year.
9. We have invited all the students in the school.
10. We have told him not to be late again.
11. They posted all the letters yesterday.

12. The machine wraps the bread automatically.
13. They paid me a lot of money to do the job.
14. Fortunately, they didn't damage the machinery.
15. We send the newspapers to Scotland by train.

Q 3. Rewrite these sentences in the passive. The subject of the active sentence can usually be omitted; you should include in the passive sentences only if it is necessary:

1. Someone's interview Dr Johnson at the moment.
   Dr Johnson_____

   Dr Johnson's being interviewed at the moment.

2. You mustn't use this machine after 5:30 p.m.
   This machine_____

3. We had warned him the day before not to go too near to the canal.
   He_____

4. They were painting the outside of the ship when the accident happened.
   The outside of the ship_____

5. You must clean this machine every time you use it.
   This machine_____

6. You should keep the flowers in a warm sunny place.
   The flowers_____

7. They're mending your shoes at the moment.
   Your shoes_____

8. Someone will drive your car to Edinburg on Tuesday.
   Your car_____

9. You should pay your bill before you leave the hotel.
   Your bill_____

10. I have told the children about the party.
    The children_____

11. About thirty million people watching this programme.
    This programme_____

12. We expect students not to talk during the examination.
    Students_____

13. You mustn't touch this button while experiment is in progress.
    This button_____

14. Someone will blow a whistle if there is a emergency.
    A whistle_____

15. Someone was carrying the bomb to a safe place when it exploded.
    The bomb_____

16. Someone's moved my chair!
    My chair_____

17. The police are questioning Mr and Mrs Davidson.
    Mr and Mrs Davidson_____

18. Someone checks the water level every week.
    The water level_____

19. We invited two hundred people to the wedding.
    Two hundred people_____

20. We don't allow smoking in this restaurant.
    Smoking ______

21. Teachers never allow talking inside a class.
    Talking __________
22. Somebody took my books and pencils.

Exercise 5

Q 1. Look at these newspaper headlines and tell your friend what's in the news. Use the passive with get in the present perfect (e.g. has got) or the present continuous (e.g. are getting).

E.g.: Post office loses important document

You: *An important document has got lost.*

1. Heavy lorries damaging motor ways
You: The motorways _______________________

2. Vandals knock wall down
You: A wall _______________________

3. Storm blows off roof
You: A roof _______________________

4. Companies paying industrial workers higher wages
You: Industrial workers _______________________

Q 2. Complete the sentences. If possible, use a tense of the verb get. Otherwise use the verb be.

1. I never found that book we were looking for. It _____ lost when we moved house
2. After the way he behaved last time he went to their house it's unlikely he _____ asked there again.
3. Naturally this vase is expensive. After all, it _____ believed to be over three hundred years old.
4. I phoned to explain what had happened but I _____ cut off before I could finish.
5. There isn't any cheese left; it _____ eaten by the children.
6. He was a well-known expert on animal diseases and his opinions _____ greatly respected.
7. The competition is stiff and be thrilled if her design _____ chosen.

8. The book _____ torn when the children started fighting over who should read it first.
9. Please don't touch anything on my desk. You _____ employed to answer the telephone, not to tidy the office.
10. She was quite friendly at first, then she _____ promoted and she doesn't care about us any more.

Q 3. Complete the sentences by using an appropriate form of <u>get</u> and the given verbs.

E.g.: I think I'll stop working. I _____ (tire).
I think I'll stop working. I am getting tired.
1. There was an accident, but nobody _____ (hurt).
2. We didn't have a map, so we _____ (lose).
3. We can't leave as soon as you _____ (dress).
4. When you _____ (marry).
5. How long did it take you to _____ (accustom) to living here?
6. Sam was supposed to be home an hour ago, but he still isn't here. I _____ (worry).
7. Just try to take it easy. Don't _____ (upset).
8. I _____ (confuse) because everybody gave me different advice.
9. We can't leave as soon as I _____ (do) with his work.
10. Chris _____ (depress) when she lost her job, so I tried to cheer her up.
11. You _____ (invite) to the party?
12. I _____ (bore), so I didn't stay for the end of the movie.
13. I'll be ready to leave as soon as I _____ (pack).
14. I _____ (pay) on I'll give you the money I owe you next Friday. Okay?
15. After Ed graduated he _____ (hire) by an engineering firm.
16. But later he _____ (fire) because he didn't do his work.
17. Last night I _____ (finish, not) with my homework until after midnight.
18. I _____ (disgust) and left because the things they were saying at the meeting were ridiculous.
19. First, they _____ (engage). Then, they _____ (marry). Later, they _____ (divorce).
20. Finally, they _____ (remarry). Today they are very happy.

Exercise 6

Q 1. Give the corresponding passive construction.

1. Everybody objected to his proposal.
2. We sent for comrade D. as soon as the telegram arrived.
3. I think that we can rely on this information.
4. They insisted on these terms.
5. They often refer to his book.
6. Everybody looked at them when they entered the hall.
7. Do you think that we can rely on these figures?
8. I'm afraid that they will not arrive at an agreement.
9. I'm sure that the newspapers will comment on this event.
10. I'm sure that nobody will object to this plan.
11. Will they listen to him with interest?
12. Did they speak much of this event?
13. They must look in to this matter.
14. You must send for them as soon as possible.
15. The contract provided for the delivery of caviar at regular intervals.
16. They must dispose of the goods in the near future.
17. You can depend on her.
18. Many facts accounted for the rise in the price of tin.
19. They may object to your plan.
20. They must comment on this event.
21. Nobody laughed at him when he said it.
22. You should refer to this quotation more often.
23. You must listen to your teacher very attentively.
24. You must not interfere with them.
25. You should not insist on it.

Q 2. Put the sentence with a verb + preposition/adverb combination into the passive.

1. The government has called out troops.
2. Fog held up the trains.
3. You are to leave this here. Someone will call for it later on.
4. We called in the police.
5. They didn't look after the children properly.
6. Then they called up the men of 28.
7. Everyone looked up to him.

8. All the ministers will see him off at the airport.
9. He hasn't slept in his bed.
10. We can build on more rooms.
11. They threw him out.
12. They will have to adopt a different attitude.
13. He's a dangerous maniac. They ought to lock him up.
14. Her story didn't take them in.
15. Burglars broke into the house.
16. The manufactures are giving away small toys with each packet of cereal.
17. They took down the notice.
18. They frown on smoking here.
19. After the government had spent a million pounds on the scheme they decided that it was impracticable and gave it up. *(Make only the first and last verbs passive.)*
20. People must hand in their weapons.
21. The crowd shouted him down.
22. People often take him for his brother.
23. No one has taken out the cork.
24. The firm company were to have used the pool for aquatic displays, but now they have changed their minds about it and are filling it in. *(Make the first and last verbs passive.)*
25. This college is already full. We are turning away the whole time.
26. You will have to pull down this skyscraper as you have not complied with the town planning regulations.

Q 3. *Express in the passive the second of each of the following pairs of sentences. Do not mention the active subjects. The first two sentences are done for you.*

Examples: 1. He seldom keeps his promise. No one can rely on him. *He can't be relied on.*

2. He's very sensitive. He doesn't like people to laugh at him. *He doesn't like to be laughed at.*

1. The child is very ill. Someone must send for the doctor.
2. The old car is in excellent condition. The owner has looked after it very well.

3. He was speaking for two hours. The people listened to him in complete silence.
4. She is going into hospital tomorrow. The doctors and nurses will take good care of her.
5. This little boy is always dirty. No one looks after him properly.
6. She is always breaking things in the kitchen. Someone must speak to her about her carelessness.
7. He's sensible man. People listen to his advise carefully.
8. The dentist said her teeth were very bad. No one had taken care of them.
9. He never broke a promise in his life. People could always rely on him.
10. Shakespeare was born more than 400 years ago. People look upon him as the greatest of English poets.

Q 4. *Give the corresponding passive construction.*

1. We looked through all advertisements very attentively
2. The gardener gathered all the dry leaves and set fire to them.
3. People will talk much about the successful debut of the young actress, no doubt.
4. You can rely upon your guide's experience.
5. Why didn't the speaker dwell longer upon this question?
6. You should send the sick man to hospital. They will look after him much better there.
7. He was very glad that nobody took notice of his late arrival.
8. He was a brilliant speaker, and, whenever he spoke, the audience listened to him with great attention.
9. Why did they laugh at him?
10. Nobody ever referred to that incident
11. U sent my daughter for the doctor.
12. We listened to the teacher very attentively.
13. We spoke much about his speech.
14. His friend always found fault with him.
15. We often refer to his article.
16. They agreed upon the plan.
17. People often ask for this book.
18. My friend always takes care of my little sister.
19. They took no notice of his words.
20. They will listen to his lectures with great interest.
21. His friends always laugh at him.

Exercise 7

Q 1. Use the notes to write sentences about American history. Put the important underlined information at the end of the sentence.

E.g.: <u>Britain</u> - rule the American colonies

The American colonies were ruled by Britain.

1. Washington - become - President
Washington_____

2. buy - Louisiana - <u>from France.</u>
Louisiana_____

discover - gold – <u>California</u>_________

<u>the North</u> - win - the Civil War   _____

black people - want - <u>equal rights</u>_________

3. shoot -Kennedy -<u>1963</u>_________

Q 2. Put the sentences into the passive voice.

1. I must do it at once.
2. You can use the material for your work.
3. I can't send off the letter today.
4. We couldn't finish the work in time.
5. You may leave the dictionaries on the table.
6. We have to do this work every day.
7. They had to put the goods on the deck.
8. The sellers are to charter a ship for the transportation of the goods.
9. You should change the end of your story.
10. The committee must discuss the question immediately.
11. The accountant mast check the invoice.
12. The manufactures can deliver the machine at the end of the month.
13. The agent must inform the buyers of the arrival of the steamer.
14. You mustn't use this machine after 5:30 p.m.
15. You should keep the flowers in a worm sunny place.

16. He must clean this machine every time he uses it.
17. You should pay your bill before you leave the hotel.
18. You mustn't touch this button while the experiment in progress.
19. The children shouldn't have opened that parcel.
20. All visitors must wear identity badges.

Q 3. Complete the sentences with the given words using them in the passive.

1. James (should + tell) the news as soon as possible.
2. James (should + tell) the news a long time ago.
3. Meat (must + keep) in a refrigerator or it will spoil.
4. We tried, but the window (couldn't + open). It was painted shut.
5. Good news! I (may + offer) a job soon. I had an interview at an engineering firm yesterday.
6. The class for next semester is too large. It (ought to + divide) in half, but there is not enough money in the budget to hire another teacher.
7. Last semester's class was too large. It (ought to +divide) in half.
8. These books (have to + return) to the library by tomorrow.
9. A: Andy, your chores (had better + finish) by the time I get home, including taking out the garbage.
   B: Don't worry, Mom. I'll do everything you told me to do.

10. Ann's birthday was on the 5th, and now it is already the 8th. Her birthday card (should + send) a week ago. May be we'd better give her a call to wish her a belated happy birthday.

Q 4. Use the verb in parentheses with any appropriate modal or similar expressions. All of the sentences are passive. In many sentences, more than one modal is possible. Use the modal that sounds best to you.

1. The entire valley (see) from their mountain home.
2. He is wearing a gold band on his fourth finger. He (marry).
3. According to our teacher, all of our compositions (write) in ink. He won't accept papers written in pencil.
4. I found this book on my desk when I came to class. It (leave) by one of the students in the earlier class.

5. Five of the committee members will be unable to attend the next meeting. In my opinion, the meeting (postpone).
6. A child (give, not) everything he or she wants.
7. Your daughter has a good voice. Her interest in singing (encourage).
8. Try to speak slowly when you give your speech. If you don't, some of your words (misunderstand).
9. Some UFO sightings (explain, not) easily. No one is able to explain them easily.

Q 5. Read this letter from Maurice, who is on holiday in Britain, to his sister Sally in New Zealand. Put the verbs in a suitable tense, active or passive.

Dear Sally,

How are you? We've been having a lovely time. We're very well looked after by our hosts. We (take) sightseeing and we (introduce) to some of their friends, who (make) us feel very welcome. Last night we (show) round a castle, by the owner! Most of the land in this area (belong) to his family for about five hundred years. Apparently, the land (give) to them after one of the his ancestors (kill) while trying to save the king's life. Quite romantic, isn't it?

The castle itself was a little bit disappointing, to be absolutely honest. The owner told us that it (suffer) serious damage during a fire about thirty years ago. When it (restore) they (add) central heating and things like that. So once you're inside it (not feel) much different to any other large, old house. But the owner is a real character. He told us lots of stories about things that (happen) to him when he was abroad to work in a bank, but he hated it, so he (behave) very badly in order to (sack). He kept us laughing for hours. I hope he (invite) here before we leave.

I'll have lots more to tell you when we get back. Take care.

Yours affectionately,

Maurice.

Exercise 8

Q 1. Rewrite these sentences in the Passive.

1. Glinka composed the opera «Ivan Susanin».
2. This mine will produce large quantities of coal this year.
3. A railway line connects the village with the town.
4. A famous architect designed this theatre.
5. This plant had fulfilled the yearly plan by the 15th November.
6. The student read the text aloud
7. The teacher will correct the student's composition.
8. Soviet scientists are making wonderful discoveries.
9. Who has written this article?
10. The workers are unloading the steamer.
11. The director has just signed the letter.
12. The customs officer is counting the cases.
13. When he entered the room, the legal adviser was checking the contract.
14. The buyers will insure the cargo with «Gosstrakh».
15. As the buyers had not opened a letter of credit, we could not ship the goods.

Q 2. Put the verb in brackets into the Past Indefinite in the Active or in the Passive Voice.

1. A note (bring) in, addressed to Eleanor, and (put) on a table to await her.
2. When the door (close), old Jolyon (drop) his paper, and (stare) long and anxiously in front of him.
3. To his knowing eyes the scene below easily (explain).
4. Then the door (shut) behind him/
5. Finally his name (call), and the boy (push) forward to her.
6. Taking the lamp, they (go) into the woodshed where the coal (deposit).
7. Finally he (persuade) by Bass to go away.
8. But when autumn (come) the cows (drive) home from the grass.
9. I (lead) the way up and as I (reach) the top, the door (open) by Mr. Smith.
10. At lunch nothing (discuss) but the latest news.
11. Bass, a very much astonished boy, (set) free.

12. «Will you work on this job all your life?» The question (ask) with sincere interest.
13. Jerry (know) he (hide) by darkness and the massive foliage. She (tap) on the door. John (open) it
14. For the few first minutes he (occupy) with eating; then as his appetite (quiet), he (take) his time.
15. The living-room (sweep), (mop) and (dust).

Q 3. Put the verb in brackets into the Past Simple, the Past Continuous and the Past Perfect in the Active or in the Passive Voice.

1. Each of the children (receive) a due share of Mrs. Gerhardt's attention. The little baby closely (look) after her.
2. From the clink of dishes one could tell that supper (prepare).
3. He (take) them out to the house, and George (show) the way to the office.
4. The front door of his house (unlock) as he (leave) it.
5. Mrs. Brown (come) to inform her that dinner already (serve).
6. His phrase (greet) by a strange laugh from a student who (sit) near the wall.
7. Jennie (leave) alone, but, the wood-dove, she (be0 a voice of sweetness in the summer-time.
8. Anne (not see) Henry until the party (seat).
9. In the meantime the evening meal (announce), and she (go) and (join) the family.
10. Lester (not attend) the wedding, though he (invite).
11. While the supper (eat) Sebastian (offer) a suggestion to go there immediately.
12. Anne (shake) by the incredible change of his tone.
13. She (want) things not so much for herself as for her child , and she (be) anxious to do whatever she (tell).
14. The house (look) after with scrupulous care by others, for Jennie (be) incapable of attending to it herself.
15. As she (come) to the carriage the door (open) and (see) a woman there.
16. When the phone (ring), I (reach) for the phone, and (tell) I (call) from Moscow.
17. In the meanwhile Jennie (leave) to brood.
18. At the very second the beautiful music she (listen) to (listen) by everyone who (be) there.
19. Mark (open) his eyes hard, (shake) his head, and (look) at the other bed. It (not sleep) in.

Q 4. Put the verb in brackets into the required tense in the Active or in the Passive Voice.

1.)

1. We constantly (disturb) by unnecessary telephone calls yesterday.
2. I (take) aback by what you (tell) me just now.
3. Tell me the truth, you (shock) by what I (say)?
4. The office (fill) with the activity of the radio show.
5. The game (play) well by both teams last Sunday.
6. Cleveland like every other growing city at this time (crowd) with those who (seek) employment.
7. At Bass's suggestion Jennie (write) her mother to come at once, and a week are or later a suitable house (find) and (rent).
8. Every morning the boys (tell0 what to do.
9. The storyteller (ask) to tell the tale again.

2)

1. When we (come) in a meal (prepare) for us.
2. What tune (play) when we (come) in?
3. I (sit) down for a rest while the shoes (repair).
4. The man (operate) on when the lights (go) out.
5. It take a moment before Nick (realise) that he (offer) a newspaper.
6. I couldn't take any photographs because my camera (repair) at that time.

3)

1. I suppose you (tell) this before.
2. Come in and have your milk. It (keep) hot for you long. You (be) late. Where you (be)?
3. It (occur) to me that for the last twenty-two hours my life (govern) by yours - by your needs.

Exercise 9 [Solved]

Q 1. Change the below sentences from Passive voice to Active voice:
1. The ball was kicked by the boy.
2. Dinner was cooked by the girl.
3. A lesson plan was written by the teacher.
4. The mailman was barked at by the dog.
5. The table was jumped on by the cat.
6. The meat was cooked by Sarath.
7. The essay was written by Salim.
8. The kennel was cleaned by the attendant.
9. The movie was directed by Christopher Nolan.
10. The chemistry book was read by the students.
11. The error was made by Andrew.
12. The rings were found by Catherine.
13. The proposal was denied by the board.
14. The book was written by Lewis Carroll.
15. The bold decision was taken by the CEO.

Q 2. Change the below sentences from Active voice to Passive voice:
1. The carpenter built the house.
2. The reckless driver drove the car.
3. My grandmother baked the cake.
4. The committee wrote the report.
5. The manager sent the email.
6. The chef is preparing a delicious meal.
7. The engineers constructed a new bridge.
8. She will complete the assignment today.
9. People speak Portuguese in that colony.
10. The tide damaged the old dam.
11. The girls are solving maths problems.
12. A thief stole my car from the garage.
13. My mother planted beautiful flowers on the lawn.
14. The school awarded Bhavana the first prize.
15. Softtech Solution has developed a new software program.

Q 3. Fill-in-the-blanks
1. The dog ___ by Sarah. [Feed/ Is fed]
2. The trophy ___ by our team this year. [Is won/Was won]
3. The students' progress ___ regularly by their class teacher. [Is checked/Check]
4. The mechanic ___ the car's engine yesterday. [Was Repaired/ Repaired]
5. She ___ a cake for the party. [Is Baking/ Was Baked]
6. You ___ with all the necessary information by them. [Will be intimated/ Intimate]
7. The weeds in the garden ___ by him. [Are being trimmed/Trim]
8. The principal ___ the student for misbehaviour. [Suspended/Is suspended]
9. The teacher ___ the lesson to the students. [Explains/ Is Explained]
10. My car ___ by myself yesterday. [Was fixed/Fixes]
11. They ___ walk-in-interviews for 15 job posts. [Are conducting/Was conducted]
12. A dacoit ___ red-handed by the villagers. [Catch/Was caught]
13. His research ___ in a scientific journal. [Will be published/Publish]
14. She ___ the managerial post by the company. [Was offered/Is offering]
15. The audience ___ the band's performance. [Applauded/ Is Applauded]
16. The team leader ___ the task to his juniors. [Has assigned/Was assigned]
17. Our cook ___ a special dish for the guests. [Is preparing/Is being prepared]
18. Several houses ___ by the storm. [Were destroyed/Destroying]
19. The election result ___ by the committee next week. [Announces/Will be announced]
20. A charity event ___. [Organising/Was organised]
21. She ___ this book to her friends. [Was recommended/Recommended]
22. Burj Khalifa ___ by Mr. Adrian Smith. [Designing/Was designed]
23. The company ___ Rohith a performance bonus. [Gave/Was given]
24. Physics rules ___ in class by the professors. [Are explained/Explaining]

25. The two brothers ___ the roof of the thatch. [Are fixing/ Was fixed]
26. The police ___ the criminal yesterday. [Is caught/Caught]
27. Devi ___ the task before Friday. [Will finish/Are finished]
28. The members ___ the beautiful sea beach. [Are cleaning/Has been cleaned]
29. The four walls of the room ___ pink by Shruthi. [Were painted/Paints]
30. One candidate ___ for the job by the committee. [Has been selected/Selecting]

Q 4. Comprehension passages

Example: Transformation from Active voice to Passive voice example:

Active Voice: We need to explore the world of science and open doors to endless possibilities. Scientists do experiments, research unnatural extraordinary things, and create theories to explain various mysteries. They explore the depths of space, investigate microscopic organisms, and uncover the intricacies of our planet.

Passive Voice:

The world of science needs to be explored to open doors to endless possibilities. Experiments are made, and research is conducted on unnatural extraordinary things and theories are created to explain various mysteries by scientists. The depths of space are explored, microscopic organisms are investigated, and the intricacies of our planet are uncovered.

Exercise:

Transform the passage from Active voice to Passive voice:

A student should be involved in some kind of sport due to its numerous benefits. If a student participates in sports activities it can nurture his/her physical fitness, enhance stamina, and strength. It implements discipline, teamwork, and leadership qualities that are crucial for personal development. It offers a platform for making new friends and building social skills.

Transformation from Passive voice to Active voice example:

Passive Voice:

The history book was read by the students in the library yesterday. The lessons were learnt, and notes were taken. Explanations were given by the teacher, and questions were asked by students.

Active Voice:
Yesterday, the students read the history book in the library. They learned the lessons and took notes. The teacher gave explanations, and students asked questions.

Exercise: Transform the passage from Passive voice to Active voice: Geography is taught by the teacher every Thursday morning. Lessons about civilizations are presented during these classes. The whiteboard is used for explanations, and questions are encouraged to be asked by the students. The teacher is respected and admired by the class due to their knowledge and engaging teaching methods. Overall, Geography is considered an important subject by the school and is taught with enthusiasm and dedication.

Answers 1:
1. The boy kicked the ball.
2. The girl cooked dinner.
3. The teacher wrote a lesson plan.
4. The dog barked at the mailman.
5. The cat jumped on the table.
6. Sarath cooked the meat.
7. Salim wrote the essay.
8. The attendant cleaned the kennel.
9. Christopher Nolan directed the movie.
10. The students read the chemistry book.
11. Andrew made the error.
12. Catherine found the rings.
13. The board denied the proposal.
14. Lewis Carroll wrote the book.
15. The CEO took the bold decision.

Answers 2:
1. The house was built by the carpenter.

2. The car was driven by the reckless driver.
3. The cake was baked by my grandmother.
4. The report was written by the committee.
5. The email was sent by the manager.
6. A delicious meal is being prepared by the chef.
7. A new bridge was constructed by the engineers.
8. The assignment will be completed by her today.
9. Portuguese is spoken in that colony by people.
10. The old dam was damaged by the tide.
11. The maths problems are being solved by the girls.
12. My car was stolen from the garage by a thief.
13. Beautiful flowers were planted on the lawn by my mother.
14. Bhavana was awarded the first prize by the school.
15. A new software program has been developed by Softtech Solution.

Answers 3:

1. Is fed
2. Is won
3. Is checked
4. Repaired
5. Is Baking
6. Will be intimated
7. Are being trimmed
8. Suspended
9. Explains
10. Was fixed
11. Are conducting
12. Was caught
13. Will be published
14. Was offered
15. Applauded
16. Has assigned
17. Is preparing
18. Were destroyed
19. Will be announced
20. Was organised
21. Recommended
22. Was designed
23. Gave
24. Are explained
25. Are fixing
26. Caught
27. Will finish
28. Are cleaning
29. Were painted
30. Has been selected

***

Exercise 10

Q 1. Convert into Passive Voice

Active: She sings a beautiful song.

Active: They clean the house every day.

Active: The company manufactures high-quality products.

Active: The teacher explains the lesson to the students.

Active: The gardener waters the plants regularly.

Active: My sister baked a cake for her birthday.

Active: He repairs the car when it's broken.

Active: The mechanic services our bikes.

Active: The children love the playground.

Active: The Father looks after their children.

Active: Boys fly kites in the garden.

Active: I open an account in the bank.

Active: Farmers grow vegetables.

Active: Sita prepares food for her husband.

Answers 2

1. Passive: Delicious meals are prepared by the chef.
2. Passive: A beautiful song is sung by her.
3. Passive: The house is cleaned every day by them.
4. Passive: High-quality products are manufactured by the company.
5. Passive: The lesson is explained to the students by the teacher.
6. Passive: The plants are watered regularly by the gardener.
7. Passive: A cake is baked for her birthday by my sister.
8. Passive: The car is repaired when he breaks it.
9. Passive: Our bikes are serviced by the mechanic.
10. Passive: The playground is loved by the children.
11. Passive: Their children are looked after by the father.
12. Passive: Kites are flown by boys in the garden.
13. Passive: An account is opened for me in the bank.
14. Passive: Vegetables are grown by the farmers.
15. Passive: A food is prepared by Sita for her husband.

Active and Passive Voice Exercises (Present Continuous Tense)

Rules for changing active to passive voice in the present continuous tense.

Active Voice Structure	**Passive Voice Structure**
Subject + am/is/are (present) + Verb-ing	Object + am/is/are (present) + being + Past Participle of the Verb
Example: She is writing a letter.	*Example:* A letter is being written by her.

Q 2: Rewrite them in passive voice using the present continuous tense.

1. Active: The chef is preparing the special dish.
2. Active: She is singing a melodious song.
3. Active: They are painting the walls of the house.
4. Active: The workers are building a new bridge.
5. Active: The team is developing the software.
6. Active: The gardener is planting the flowers in the garden.
7. Active: The technician is fixing the computer.
8. Active: My mother is cooking dinner in the kitchen.
9. Active: The students are presenting their projects to the class.
10. Active: The company is launching a new product.
11. Active: She is preparing food for her husband.
12. Active: Boys are flying kites in the garden.
13. Active: Farmers are growing vegetables.
14. Active: Parents are looking after their children.
15. Active: Students are doing their work.

Answers 02:

1. Passive: The special dish is being prepared by the chef.
2. Passive: A melodious song is being sung by her.
3. Passive: The walls of the house are being painted by them.
4. Passive: A new bridge is being built by the workers.
5. Passive: The software is being developed by the team.

6. Passive: The flowers in the garden are being planted by the gardener.
7. Passive: The computer is being fixed by the technician.
8. Passive: Dinner is being cooked in the kitchen by my mother.
9. Passive: The projects are being presented to the class by the students.
10. Passive: A new product is being launched by the company.
11. Passive: A food is being prepared by Sita for her husband.
12. Passive: Kites are being flown by the boys in the garden.
13. Passive: Vegetables are being grown by the farmers.
14. Passive: The children are being looked after by their parents.
15. Passive: Their work is being done by the students.

Active and Passive Voice Exercises (Present Perfect Tense)
Rules for changing active to passive voice in the present perfect tense.

Active Voice Structure	**Passive Voice Structure**
Subject + has/have (present perfect) + Past Participle	Object + has/have (present perfect) + been + Past Participle of the Verb
Example: They have completed the project.	*Example:* The project has been completed by them.

Q 3: The following sentences are given in active voice, and you need to rewrite them in passive voice using the present perfect tense.

1. Active: They have completed the project.
2. Active: She has written a novel.
3. Active: The chef has prepared a delicious meal.
4. Active: The company has launched a new website.
5. Active: He has fixed the broken window.
6. Active: The team has won the championship.
7. Active: I have painted the living room.
8. Active: The gardener has planted new flowers in the garden.
9. Active: They have built a new playground.
10. Active: She has organized the event.
11. Active: She has prepared food for her husband.
12. Active: I have opened an account in the bank.

13. Active: Farmers have grown vegetables.
14. Active: Boys have completed their work.
15. Active: She has completed her Science project.

Answers 3

Now, here are the passive-voice versions of the sentences for your reference:

1. Passive: The project has been completed by them.
2. Passive: A novel has been written by her.
3. Passive: A delicious meal has been prepared by the chef.
4. Passive: A new website has been launched by the company.
5. Passive: The broken window has been fixed by him.
6. Passive: The championship has been won by the team.
7. Passive: The living room has been painted by me.
8. Passive: New flowers have been planted in the garden by the gardener.
9. Passive: A new playground has been built by them.
10. Passive: The event has been organized by her.
11. Passive: A food has been prepared by her for her husband.
12. Passive: An account has been opened by me in the bank.
13. Passive: Vegetables have been grown by the farmers.
14. Passive: Their work has been completed by the boys.
15. Passive: Her Science project has been completed by her.

Rules for changing active to passive voice in the past simple tense.

Active Voice Structure	**Passive Voice Structure**
Subject + Verb (past) + Object	Object + was/were (past) + Past Participle of the Verb
Example: She wrote a letter.	*Example:* A letter was written by her.

Q 4: Change to passive voice in the simple past tense.

1. Active: She wrote a letter.
2. Active: They built a house.
3. Active: He painted the fence.

4. Active: The chef cooked a delicious meal.
5. Active: Someone stole my wallet.
6. Active: The team won the championship.
7. Active: The company launched a new product last year.
8. Active: She finished the project on time.
9. Active: She wrote an interesting book.
10. Active: The company launched a new website.
11. Active: My mother cooked dinner in the kitchen.
12. Active: I opened an account in the bank.
13. Active: Boys played football in the garden.
14. Active: The thief stole my purse.
15. Active: She prepared a wonderful dish.

Answers 04

1. Passive: A letter was written by her.
2. Passive: A house was built by them.
3. Passive: The fence was painted by him.
4. Passive: A delicious meal was cooked by the chef.
5. Passive: My wallet was stolen by someone.
6. Passive: The championship was won by the team.
7. Passive: A new product was launched by the company last year.
8. Passive: The project was finished on time by her.
9. Passive: An interesting book was written by her.
10. Passive: A new website was launched by the company.
11. Passive: A dinner was cooked by my mother in the kitchen.
12. Passive: An account was opened for me in the bank.
13. Passive: A football was played by the boys in the garden.
14. Passive: My purse was stolen by the thief.
15. Passive: A wonderful dish was prepared by her.

Rules for changing active to passive voice in the past continuous tense.

Active Voice Structure	**Passive Voice Structure**
Subject + was/were (past) + Verb-ing + Object	Object + was/were (past) + being + Past Participle of the Verb
Example: She was writing a letter.	*Example:* A letter was being written by

her.

Q 5: Convert the following sentences from active voice to passive voice in the past continuous tense.

1.   Active: She was writing a letter.
2.   Active: They were building a house.
3.   Active: He was painting the fence.
4.   Active: The chef was cooking a delicious meal.
5.   Active: Someone was stealing my wallet.
6.   Active: The team was winning the championship.
7.   Active: The company was launching a new product last year.
8.   Active: She was finishing the project on time.
9.   Active: She was writing an interesting book.
10.   Active: A company was launching a new website.
11.   Active: My mother was cooking dinner in the kitchen.
12.   Active: I was opening an account in the bank.
13.   Active: Boys were playing football in the garden.
14.   Active: The children were preparing their project.
15.   Active: I was preparing a dish.

Answers 05

1.   Passive: A letter was being written by her.
2.   Passive: A house was being built by them.
3.   Passive: The fence was being painted by him.
4.   Passive: A delicious meal was being cooked by the chef.
5.   Passive: My wallet was being stolen by someone.
6.   Passive: The championship was being won by the team.
7.   Passive: A new product was being launched by the company last year.
8.   Passive: The project was being finished on time by her.
9.   Passive: An interesting book was being written by her.
10.   Passive: A new website was being launched by the company.
11.   Passive: A dinner was being cooked by my mother in the kitchen.
12.   Passive: An account was being opened by me in the bank.
13.   Passive: A football was being played by the boys in the garden.
14.   Passive: Their project was being prepared by the children.
15.   Passive: A dish was being prepared by me.

Exercise 11

Rules of Active and Passive Voice with examples for Present Simple.

Active Voice	Passive Voice (Auxiliary Verb – is/am/are)
Subject + V1+s/es+ object	Object+ is/am/are+ V3+ by + subject
Subject + Do/does+ not + V1 + Object	Object + is/am/are+ not + V3+ by Subject
Does+ Subject+ V1+Object+?	Is/am/are + Object+ V3+ by subject +?

Active and Passive Voice Example with Answers of Present Simple Tense

Active: He reads a novel.   Passive: A novel is read.
Active: He does not cook food. Passive: Food is not cooked by him.
Active: Does he purchase books?
Passive: Are books purchased by him?
Active: They grow plants.   Passive: Plants are grown by them.
Active: She teaches me.   Passive: I am taught by her.
Active: He helps me.   Passive: I am helped by him.
Active: Ravi brings the car.   Passive: The car is brought by Ravi.
Active: Snehal teaches English. Passive: …………………………
Active: Mohit walks on road.   Passive: …………………………
Active: ………………………   Passive: The ball is caught by Ravi.
Active: ………………………   Passive: Sumit is backed by Monika.

Active and Passive Voice Rules for Present Continuous Tense

Active Voice	Passive Voice (Auxiliary Verb- is/am/are + being)
Subject + is/am/are+ v1+ ing + object	Object+ is/am/are+ being+ V3+ by + subject
Subject + is/am/are+ not+ v1+ ing+ object	Object + is/am/are+ not + being+V3+ by Subject
Is/am/are+ subject+v1+ing + object+?	Is/am/are + Object+ V3+ by subject +?

Active and Passive Voice Exercises of Present Continuous Tense

Active: Esha is singing a song.
Passive: A song is being sung by Esha.

Active: Kritika is not chopping vegetables.
Passive: Vegetables are not being chopped by Kritika.

Active: Is Ritika buying a table?
Passive: Is a table being bought by Ritika?

Active: They are serving poor people.
Passive: Poor people are being served by them.

Active: She is disturbing Dinesh.
Passive: Dinesh is being disturbed by her.

Active and Passive Voice Rules for Present Perfect Tense

Active Voice	Passive Voice (Auxiliary Verb- has/have +been)
Subject + has/have+ v3+ object	Object+ has/have+ been+ V3+ by + subject
Subject + has/have+ not+ v3+ object	Object + has/have+ not + been+V3+ by Subject
Has/have+ subject+ v3 + object+?	Has/Have + Object+ been+V3+ by subject +?

Active: Nitesh has challenged her.
Passive: ………………………………………..
Active: Radhika has not written an article.
Passive: ………………………………………..
Active: Have they left the apartment?
Passive: ………………………………………..
Active: She has created this masterpiece.
Passive: ………………………………………..
Active: I have read the newspaper.
Passive: ………………………………………..
Answer:
She has been challenged by Nitesh.
An article has not been written by Radhika.
Has apartment been left by them?
This masterpiece has been created by her.
The newspaper has been read by me.

Active and Passive Voice Rules for Past Simple Tense

Active Voice	Passive Voice (Auxiliary Verb- was/were)
Subject + V2+ object	Object+ was/were V3+ by + subject
Subject +did+ not+v1+ object	Object + was/were+ not +V3+ by Subject
Did+ subject+V1+ object+?	Was/were + Object+ V3+ by subject +?

Active: Reema cleaned the floor.
Active: Aisha bought a bicycle.
Active: Naman called my friends.
Active: I saved him.
Active: Miraya paid the bills.
Active: Ravi cleared all dues of the grocer.
Active: Nikhil sailed the ship during the entire trip.
Active: Somlal saved his friends from a beast.

Answers:
Passive: The floor was cleaned by Reema.
Passive: A bicycle was bought by Aisha.
Passive: My friends were called by Naman.
Passive: He was saved by me.
Passive: The bills were paid by Miraya.
Passive: ....
Passive: ....
Passive: ....

Active and Passive Voice Rules for Past Continuous Tense

Active Voice	Passive Voice (Auxiliary Verb- was/were + being)
Subject + was/were + v1+ing+ object.	Object+ was/were +being+V3+ by + subject
Subject +was/were+ not+v1+ing + object	Object + was/were+ not +being+V3+ by Subject
Was/were+ Subject + V1+ing + object+?	Was/were + Object+ being+v3+ by+ subject+?

Active and Passive Voice Examples with Answers of Past Continuous Tense

Active: Nitika was painting the wall.
Active: Manish was repairing the car.
Active: Were you reciting the poem?
Active: She was baking the cake.
Active: She was watching me.
Active: Nikhil was playing football.
Active: Sonalika was cooking food in kitchen.

Answers:
Passive: The wall was being painted by Nitika.
Passive: The car was being repaired by Manish.
Passive: Was the poem being recited?
Passive: The cake was being baked by her.
Passive: I was being watched by her.
Passive: The football was being played by Nikhil.
Passive: ....

Active and Passive Voice Rules for Past Perfect Tense

Active Voice	Passive Voice (Auxiliary Verb- had +been)
Subject + had + v3+ object.	Object+ had+been +V3+ by + subject
Subject +had+ not+v3+ object	Object + had+ not +been+V3+ by Subject
Had+ Subject + V3+ object+?	Had + Object+ been+v3+ by+ subject+?

Active and Passive Voice Exercises of Past Perfect Tense

Active: Misha had cleaned the floor.
Active: Vidhi had not received the parcel.
Active: Vishal had solved the doubt.
Active: Had they caught the thief?
Active: I had paid fifty thousand.
Active: Soma had sailed the boat in deep sea.
Active: Had Soma sailed the beat in deep sea?
Active: Rina had cleared all her dues in the grocer.

Answers:
Passive: The floor had been cleaned by Misha.
Passive: The parcel had not been received by Vidhi.
Passive: The doubt had been solved.
Passive: Had the thief been caught by them?
Passive: Fifty thousand had been paid by me.
Passive: ………………………………………
Passive: ………………………………………
Passive: ………………………………………

Active and Passive Voice Rules for Future Simple Tense

Active Voice	Passive Voice (Auxiliary Verb- will+ be)
Subject + will+ v1+ object.	Object+ will+ be +V3+ by + subject
Subject +will + not+ V1+object	Object + will+ not +be+V3+ by Subject
Will+ Subject + V1+ object+?	Will + Object+ be +v3+ by+ subject+?

Active: Kriya will sew the bag.

Passive: The bag will be sewed by Kriya.

Active: Disha will not arrange the things.

Passive: The things will not be arranged by Disha.

Active: Will you mop the floor?

Passive: Will the floor be mopped by you?

Active: They will post the letter.

Passive: The letter will be posted.

Active: Reena will save money.

Passive: Money will be saved by Reena.

Active: Sonalika will sail the boat in deep sea.

Assive: ....

Active: Will Sonalika sail the boat in deep sea?

Assive: ....

Active: Assignments will be solved by Nikita, Ravi and Reena jointy.

Assive: ....

Active: Amit and Sumit will jointly play the title.

Assive: ....

Active: Antara will finish the race before time.

Assive: ....

Active and Passive Voice Rules for Future Perfect Tense

Active Voice	Passive Voice
Subject + will+ have +v3+ object.	Object+ will+ have+ been +V3+ by + subject
Subject + will+ have +not+v3+ object.	Object + will+ have +not+been+v3+ subject
Will+ Subject+have+v3+ object+?	Will + object+have+been+v3+by +subject+?

Active: They will have brought the toy.
Active: Nimesh will not have changed the table cover.
Active: Will she have written the notes.
Active: They will have won the match.
Active: Vijay will have washed a shirt.
Answers:
Passive: The toy will have been brought by them.
Passive: The table cover will not have been changed by Nimesh.
Passive: Will the notes have been written by her?
Passive: The match will have been won by them.
Passive: A shirt will have been washed by Vijay.

N.B. ....Use the active voice when you want to emphasize the doer of the action and make your writing more direct, clear, and concise. First you need to identify the subject, the verb, and the object: S+V+O. The second is to change the object into a subject. Thirdly, the active verb does not have an object therefore, the passive form should begin with you. If the focus is on the object, passive voice can be used. To Avoid Naming the Doer: If the doer is unknown or unimportant, passive voice can be used. Passive voice can be used to create a more formal or objective tone.

Exercise 12

Active and Passive Voice Exercises (Past Perfect Tense)
Rules for changing active to passive voice in the past perfect tense.

Active Voice Structure	Passive Voice Structure
Subject + had (past perfect) + Past Participle	Object + had (past perfect) + been + Past Participle of the Verb
Example: She had completed the project.	*Example:* The project had been completed by her.

Q 1: Convert from active voice to passive voice in the past perfect tense.

1. Active: She had completed the assignment.
2. Active: They had fixed the car.
3. Active: He had sold the house.
4. Active: The chef had prepared a delicious meal.
5. Active: Someone had stolen my wallet.
6. Active: The team had won the championship.
7. Active: The company launched a new product last year.
8. Active: She had finished the project on time.
9. Active: They had built a new playground.
10. Active: She had organized the event.
11. Active: She had prepared food for her husband.
12. Active: I had opened an account in the bank.
13. Active: Farmers had grown vegetables.
14. Active: Boys had completed their work.
15. Active: She had completed her Science project.

Answers 01

1. Passive: The assignment had been completed by her.
2. Passive: The car had been fixed by them.
3. Passive: The house had been sold by him.
4. Passive: A delicious meal had been prepared by the chef.
5. Passive: My wallet had been stolen by someone.
6. Passive: The championship had been won by the team.

7. Passive: A new product had been launched by the company last year.
8. Passive: The project had been finished on time by her.
9. Passive: A new playground had been built by them.
10. Passive: The event had been organized by her.
11. Passive: A food had been prepared by her for her husband.
12. Passive: An account had been opened by me in the bank.
13. Passive: Vegetables had been grown by the farmers.
14. Passive: Their work had been completed by the boys.
15. Passive: Her Science project had been completed by her.

Active and Passive Voice Exercises (Simple Future Tense)

Rules for changing active to passive voice in the past continuous tense.

Active Voice Structure	Passive Voice Structure
Subject + will/shall (future) + Verb	Object + will/shall (future) + be + Past Participle of Verb

Example: She will write a book. *Example:* A book will be written by her.

Q 2. Convert to passive voice in the simple future tense.

1. Active: She will write a letter.
2. Active: They will build a house.
3. Active: He will paint the fence.
4. Active: The chef will cook a delicious meal.
5. Active: Someone will steal my wallet.
6. Active: The team will win the championship.
7. Active: The company will launch a new product next month.
8. Active: She will finish the project on time.
9. Active: He will repair the car when it's broken.
10. Active: The mechanic will service our bikes.
11. Active: The children will love the playground.
12. Active: The father will look after their children.
13. Active: Boys will fly kites in the garden.
14. Active: I will open an account in the bank.
15. Active: Farmers will grow vegetables

Answers 02

1. Passive: A letter will be written by her.
2. Passive: A house will be built by them.
3. Passive: The fence will be painted by him.
4. Passive: A delicious meal will be cooked by the chef.
5. Passive: My wallet will be stolen by someone.
6. Passive: The championship will be won by the team.
7. Passive: A new product will be launched by the company next month.
8. Passive: The project will be finished on time by her.
9. Passive: The car will be repaired when he breaks it.
10. Passive: Our bikes will be serviced by the mechanic.
11. Passive: The playground will be loved by the children.
12. Passive: Their children will be looked after by the father.
13. Passive: Kites will be flown by boys in the garden.
14. Passive: An account will be opened for me in the bank.
15. Passive: Vegetables will be grown by the farmers.

***

Integrated Exercise

Exercise 1

A section of an article is given. Here some words and some sentences are missing. You need to comprehend the paragraphs and find out the suitable word/ sentence, from the provided options, which fulfill the blank grammatically and contextually correct.

Capitalism, as it is ___________(1) in rich countries, has taken two brilliant ideas too far. The first is
return on equity (ROE), one way of measuring value creation that has managed to eclipse many other, and broader, ones. The second is competition, which has come to be seen as an end in it rather than as a tool for promoting growth and _______________(2).

Both ideas began as effective solutions to a pressing problem—how to allocate resources to produce, as Jeremy Bentham would have it, "the greatest good for the greatest number." Centuries on, the ___________(3) economies _________(4) tightly to these approaches, but the problem has changed. The mismatch has caused difficulties of such urgency that many people are now declaring capitalism a ___________(5). The whole system has been ___________(6), not only because of the financial crisis but particularly since that event, as inherently unworkable.

It isn't true. Capitalism—broadly, private ownership and resources allocated by markets—remains the most powerful, flexible, and ________(7) system for driving society's prosperity and enhancing the quality of life. But keeping it on track will depend on our ability to rethink the priorities that guide everyone in the system, from entrepreneurs to regulators to investors. Together the practitioners of capitalism will need to ___________(8) the headlong pursuits of ROE and competition, and that process begins with recognizing those ideas for what they are. They are runaways.

The concept of "runaway" selection comes from the field of evolutionary biology, and to explain it, biologists most often cite the peacock's tail. That ornamental feature has grown ever more ______________(9) across the centuries thanks to a simple fact: Peahens show a preference for large-tailed peacocks. In the earliest days of the species, this made sense. A showy tail was a marker of a healthy male that knew how to feed himself. Consequently, well-feathered males had more frequent opportunities to breed and to pass along that trait. The next generation had, on average, larger tails. Initially, this would have ______________(10) the weak; but after many generations, it created a problem for the strong. That tail is expensive. It requires nutrients to grow and maintain. And it's heavy, slowing down its owner and making him easier prey.

1-

I- Practiced	II- Hinged	III- Maneuver
IV- Steered	V- None of the above	

Solution: I Hinges means attached or joint with. Maneuver is a noun where as sentence needs a verb. Steered means guide or control the movement which cannot be fit in the sentence and only practiced is the correct form of verb and grammatically fits in the sentence so option I is the right choice.

2-

I- Destruction	II- Stagnation	III- Innovation
IV- Both I and II fit	V- None of the above	

Solution: III we cannot promote destruction and stagnation so they can be easily eliminated. Only option III is the right choice.

3-

I- Advanced	II- Progressive	III- Hinder
IV- Both I and II fit	V- Both II and III fit	

Solution: IV hinder is a negative term and if we are using approaches it should be advanced and progressive both which grammatically fits in the sentence.

4-

I- Hold on

II- Grasp

III- Cling

IV- None of the above

V- All of the above

Solution: V as hold on, grasp, cling have the same meaning we can use all as the sentence is also saying advanced economies hold these approaches for centuries.

5-

I- Success

II- Achievement

III- Failure

IV- Defeat

V- None of the above

Solution: III if there is a mismatch or difficulty capitalism will not be a success or achievement it must be a failure. Defeat will not fit grammatically in the sentence.

6-

I- Indicted

II- Obsequious

III- Pristine

IV- Facile

V- None of the above

Solution: I in the above options only indicted is grammatically correct because with has been we use third form of verb and indicted means accused of something which is also logically correct so option I is the right choice.

7-

I- Fragile

II- Impotent

III- Robust

IV- Tough

V- Lethargic

Solution: III fragile impotent and lethargic are negative words which is not a case here. Tough is not used with system here. So robust is the only right choice. Robust means vigorous.

8-

I- Ennui   II- Inveigle   III- Cajole
IV- Throttle back   V- None of the above

Solution: IV ennui means a feeling of listlessness and dissatisfaction. Inveigle and cajole means to persuade someone to do something. Throttle back means to reduce the speed. And according to the sentence practitioner have to slow down the pursuits and competition to move forward effectively.

9-

I- Flamboyant   II- Ostentatious
III- Apathetic   IV- Both I and II   V- None of the above

Solution: I apathetic means which shows no interest which is not the case here. Ostentatious and flamboyant both means tending to attract attention but ostentatious is used when we pretend to attract someone and flamboyant is used when it is attracted based on its characteristics. So flamboyant is the only right choice. Thus option I is correct.

10-

I- Strengthened II- Beefed up
III- Enlarged   IV- None of the given options   V- Weeded out

Solution: V weed out means to remove which fits in the sentence, hence option V is the right choice.

.

Exercise 2

Directions: In this exercise, the dialogue between two people is jumbled in four parts, i.e. 1, 2, 3 and 4. Arrange these jumbled sentences into a logical order to make a meaningful dialogue.

Q 1.
1. "Oh my God! What about your Father? Any sign of him?
2. "No Mum, just the trolley. Shall we go out and see if we can find him?
3. No! Whatever happens, we must stay here. It's a trap." Those lights are there to lure us out."
4. "Mum, come quick! The big people have found Dad's shopping trolley and put it on their table next to two huge lights."
a. 2134   b. 4123   c. 4321   d. 1243

Q 2.
1. "Apparently they've just introduced a second security gate."
2. "Couple of days, what about you?"
3. "Been here long mate?"
4. "Just arrived. Any idea what's causing the queue?
a 2314   b. 1324   c. 2341   d. 3241

Q 3.
1. "A treat I think Charlie. We did a trick last time."
2. "There's the front doorbell again Charlie. must be the third time tonight. It'll be more youngsters I expect, out 'Trick or Treating'. Shall I go, or will you?"
3. "OK my sweetheart a treat it shall be. How many would you like?"
4. "I'll go love, you have a rest and finish off your cup of tea. What shall we do this time, trick or treat?"
a. 2143   b. 1324   c. 2413   d. 1234

Q 4.

1. "Just want to let you know kid, in case you were wondering, that last cake, the chocolate éclair, it's got my name on it. Touch it and I'll have your fingers off!"
2. "Well kid, it's up to you. What's it going to be, cake or fingers?"
3. "Mum, mum, Aunt Sally's dog just said he's gong to bite me. He says the chocolate éclair's his."
4. "Don't be silly dear, little Henry can't talk, he's a dog. Now play nicely with him, there's a darling. And don't feed him any of your cake, Aunt Sally has got him on a strict diet."

a. 1342 b. 2341 c. 1432 d. 2314

Q 5.
1. "It depends. How heavy are you? 'Cos my Dad says I'm not big enough to lift heavy things."
2. "I'm 14 pounds, give or take a few ounces. If you can't lift me, just drag me to the edge and push me over the side. Please."
3. "No! Don't go. I'm sorry. It's being stranded here on this pier that's making me grumpy. I'm getting a bit short of breath and this sun is starting to dry me out. If you could help me back into the water I'd be extremely grateful."
4. "No need to be rude Mister, I was only asking. My Dad says rude people should be ignored. I wonder if the same goes for rude fish? I think it probably does, I'm off."

a. 1243 b. 4312 c. 3214   d. 2134

Q 6.
1. "Keep your voice down Billy, he'll hear you."
2. "He won't like that mate. You know what he's like. Nobody ever leaves, not of their own accord anyway. Why don't you just finish your meal. You'll feel better afterwards."
3. "He won't like that mate. You know what he's like. Nobody ever leaves, not of their own accord anyway. Why don't you just finish your meal. You'll feel better afterwards."
4. "I don't care. I'm telling you, things need to change round here, or I'm off."

a. 1243 b. 4231 c. 3214 d. 2143

Q 7.

1. "Looks like we've found them, sir."

2. "It's a family unit, sir. A female, a male and two young siblings. Our probes indicate that they are the right age and relatively well preserved."

3. "Thank goodness for that Captain. I wasn't looking forward to having to report to the authorities that our mission had failed. What exactly have you got?"

4. "Excellent Captain. How long before we have them securely on board?"

a. 4321 b. 2134 c.1324   d. 1342

Q 8.

1. "Seems the driver leant out of the car screaming at everyone to get out of his way. Started honking his horn. There was panic. That's when that fiery young lamb, Jake leapt at him and tore off his arm. Blood everywhere."

2. "Not sure mate. Someone says the idiot in the car wouldn't slow down. Seems he hit the old ewe, Matilda. You know, her with the dodgy back legs. She never stood a chance."

3. "Then what? I just heard the screams. That's when I started running."

4. "What's happened Joe?"

a. 1323 b. 4231 c. 1324 d. 1243

Q 9.

1. "But kids, it's really important. I need all the help I can get and we haven't got much time left. I thought I felt some rain as I was coming in. This could be it."

2. "Noah, leave the children be and stop scaring them. Get back to your boat building and I'll come out and give you a hand after tea. And Noah... please take that silly helmet off, you're going to frighten the neighbours."

3. Dad, leave us alone. We're having fun building dens. We keep telling you, we don't want to help you outside!"

4. "Mum! Dad's being weird again."

a. 3142 b. 4231 c. 1324 d. 1234

Q 10.

1. "No idea mate. I just process things this end. My job's to make sure you leave your clothes and any other earthly possessions here before you go down the hole. A bloke called Peter will meet you at the bottom and send you on your way."

2. This morning, I think. I remember crossing the road outside my office, hearing the sreech of brakes then nothing. Next thing I know I'm in this queue."

3. "According to my list you should've been knocked down by that lorry yesterday morning not today. Bloody typical of the Grim Reaper, always messing up his timings. Still you're here now. Get you're clothes off, you're next."

4. "But where am I going?"

a. 3214 b. 2341 c. 1243 d. 2413

Answers

Q 1: 4123	Q 2: 3241	Q 3: 2413
Q 4: 1342	Q 5: 4312	Q 6: 2143
Q 7: 1324	Q 8: 4231	Q 9: 3142
Q 10: 2341		

Exercise 3

Here is the example of <u>cloze test</u>.[17] First try to solve the answers by yourself and than check with solutions.

Hardly had I boarded a bus for the railway station when, to my dismay, I remembered that I had forgotten my purse at home. If ever you have had such an experience, you will find know the feeling which such a discovery ___(1)_____ . In such a situation, one would be _____(2)____ because he would look like a fool at the best and like a ____(3)__ at the worst. One would not be at all ___(4)___ if the conductor gavee you a contemptuous stare as much as to say, " Yes , I know that ___(5)___old trick, Now then, you be ____(6)__ the bus", and even if the conductor were, a ___(7)___ fellow and allowed you to travel without paying the fare, you would still be faced with the necessity of going back home to collect your purse and thus ___(8)__ the train. Having searched my pockets in ___(9)___ for stray coins and having found I was ___(10)__ penniless, I told the conductor with as honest a face as I could assume that I couldn't pay the fare, and must go back for money.

1)   a. acquires   b. arouses   c. creates   d. shows   e. imparts

2)   a. annoyed   b. happy   c. pained   d. pleased   e. miserable

3)   a. gullible   b. half-witted   c. knave   d.simpleton   e. idiot

4)   a. angry   b. annoyed   c. satisfied   d. surprised   e. happy

---

5)   a. clever b. fresh   c. stale   d. ugly   e. cunning

6)   a. board b. leave c. off   d. stand   e. sit

7)   a. bad   b. good   c. harsh   d. strict   e. rash

8) a. boarding b.catching   c. meeting d. missing   e. stopping

9) a. anxiety b. vain c. hurry   d. desperation e. hopelessness

10) a. utterly   b. mostly   c. partially   d. truly   e. totally

Solution
1) b. arouses - emotions, feelings and responses

2) a. annoyed - impatient or angry

3) c. Knave - jack of face cards

4) d. surprised - amazed or stunned

5) c. stale - day-old or unoriginal

6) c. off - from a particular thing or place

7) b. good - positive quality

8) d. missing - fail to reach or get to on time

9) b. vain - immoderate or overstated sense

10) a. utterly - absolutely

Exercise 4

In the following passage, there are words highlighted and has been numbered. these numbers are printed below the passage and against each, four words are given and marked as A, B, C and D out of which only one word fits the blank. Incase if the given word itself is appropriate then Mark the option E as the answer

It is becoming increasingly fashionable to tax the super-rich. Taxing the super rich primarily involves (1) <u>channelising</u> the rates of personal income tax or property taxes. It ignores what actually happens with the incomes of the super- rich. Higher expenditure on goods and services results in more revenue being (2) <u>generated</u> through indirect taxes. Moreover if taxes are low, there is no incentive to (3) <u>trade</u> either income or the acquisition of goods and services. Beyond a point, most income is then invested in financial institutions which, in turn, help fuel industrial and economic growth.

It is axiomatic that a small percentage of the population in any country will always control a major portion of its wealth. The top five percent will always earn more than fifty percent of the total income and generate most of nation's wealth. (4) <u>incoherently</u> taxing this class will result in the (5) <u>alienation</u> of a class of the dishonest rich. If a man cannot become rich honestly, he will do so dishonestly. Alternatively, if he has a sense of values and ethics, he has no option but to escape to other countries. The (6) <u>migration</u> of a large number of India's brightest engineers and doctors was in no small measure due to our socialist principles and heavy taxes.

The (7) <u>penultimate</u> of the tax system is that the honest tax payer is (8) <u>favourably</u> attacked again and again. The dishonest tax payer (9) <u>judiciously</u> pays his tax dues. If the goal is to earn greater revenue, then taxing the super-rich will be counter productive. The marginal gain in revenue will be temporary and there will be greater loss of revenue through (10) <u>alarming</u> collection of indirect taxes. Hence it is necessary to re examine these myriad wasteful welfare schemes.

1.

A. Truncating   B. Increasing   C. Focusing
D. Reducing   E. No changes required

2.
A. Derived   B. Lowered   C. Validated
D. Propagated   E. No changes required

3.
A. Merge   B. Explore   C. Violate
D. Conceal   E. No changes required

4.
A. Heavily   B. Marginally   C. Temporarily
D. partially   E. No changes required

5.
A. Defamation   B. Creation   C. Transition
D. Suppression   E. No changes required

6.
A. Attrition   B. Termination   C. Retention
D. Coalition   E. No changes required

7.
A. Probation   B. Tragedy   C. Charge
D. Incentive   E. No changes required

8.
A. Savagely   B. Earnestly   C. Hardly
D. Visually   E. No changes required

9.
A. Actively   B. Always   C. Seldom
D. Secretly   E. No changes required

10.
A. Startling   B. Regaining   C. Reassuring

D. Worsening   E. No changes required

Answer with Explanation

1. Option B
By skimming through the passage it is clear that the theme of the passage is about taxing super rich people in the society.
From the very first sentence truncating, reducing and channelising cannot be the answer. All the above-mentioned words have a similar meaning. By substituting focusing and increasing in the blank, increasing perfectly fits the sentence.

2. Option E
Validated means to check. Propagate means to spread widely. Derived means to obtain something from. Generated means to produce. Here revenue cannot be either propagated, derived or validated. Only possible word which perfectly fits the blank will be generated.

3. Option D
Merge means to combine; Explore means to evaluate
Violate means fail to respect; Conceal means to keep secret
Here trade, explore and merge cannot be the answer.word conceal fits the sentence appropriately

4. Option A
Partially, temporarily and marginally can be Eliminated. Incoherently means illogically. While substituting incoherently and heavily in the sentence, the word heavily gives perfect meaning to the sentence.

5. Option B
Defamation means damaging good name of a person
Alienation means transfer of ownership of property rights
Transition means process of changing from one state to another
Suppression means to suppress
Defamation and suppression gives opposite meaning to the sentence. Alienation and transition cannot be the answer since it doesn't fit the sentence, therefore the word creation will be the answer.

6. Option E

Retention gives opposite meaning, so it is Eliminated.

Attrition means process of reducing something

Termination means to stop. Coalition means temporary alliance for combined action. Migration means movement of people from one place to another place. From the above four words migration gives the perfect meaning to the sentence.

7. Option B

Probation, charge and incentive can be Eliminated

Penultimate means last but one in a series, which doesn't give meaning to the sentence. Since the sentence implies negative meaning tragedy Will be the perfect answer.

8. Option A

Visually and favourably gives opposite meaning to the sentence. Word hardly can't be the answer. Savagely means uncontrolled manner. Earnestly means seriously

Among the above 2 words savagely gives appropriate meaning to the sentence.

9. Option C

Actively, always and judiciously gives opposite meaning to the sentence. Word Secretly can be Eliminated.

Seldom means rarely, which will be the perfect answer to the sentence.

10. Option A

Regaining, Reassuring give opposite negative meanings. Worsening means to make or become worse. Among the other three words, Startling fits the sentence properly.

Exercise 5

Which of the phrases given below each sentence should replace the phrase printed in bold type to make the sentence grammatically correct? If the sentence is correct as it is, mark 'E' as the answer.

1. Less than a million of rupees are required immediately. Go to the bank and withdraw the cash.

A. rupees were   B. rupees was   C. rupees to be

D. rupees is   E. No correction required

2. Soup and Salad are a wholesome food.

A. are   B. are not   C. may be a

D. is a   E. No correction required

3. I as well as my mother are going to attend the meeting.

A. am going   B. is going   C. were going

D. had been going   E. No correction required

4. A mango is considered the king among fruits.

A. An apple   B. An mango

C. A apple   D. The mango

E. No correction required

5. He bought ten dozens of bananas.

A. large quantity   B. plenty of

C. ten dozen   D. did not bought

E. No correction required

6. I want one of the book kept on the table.

A. this very book   B. any book

C. one of the books   D. no book

E. No correction required

7. I have been working for this institute since four months.

A. for four months   B. for 4 months

C. less than 4 months   D. not for four months

E. No correction required

8. Sonia Gandhi has been ill for last Monday.

A. is ill for last   B. was ill for last

C. has been ill since last   D. had been ill for last

E. No correction required

9. Pune is certain to win the IPL series.
A. most likely   B. not likely   C. impossible
D. probably   E. No correction required

10. Walk slowly lest you should not fall.
A. fast lest you should not   B. fast lest you should
C. slowly lest you should   D. slowly and you should
E. No correction required

Solution

Answer 1: Option D.
Explanation: Whenever adjectives such as much, less, little and more are used as nouns, they are always followed by a singular verb. Another Example: A little of good habits makes our life happy – is the correct sentence.

Answer 2: Option D.
Explanation: If two subjects express one common idea, it is always followed by a singular verb. Another Example: Bread and Butter is a good breakfast – is the correct sentence.

Answer 3: Option A.
Explanation: If two subjects are joined together by as well as; then the verb in the sentence will always be according to the first subject. Another Example: He as well as his brothers is sitting in the park – is the correct sentence.
Answer 4: Option D.
Explanation: Whenever a singular noun represents the whole class, then "The" is used before it. Another Example: The ass is used as a beast of burden – is the correct sentence. But remember "Man" and "Woman" do not take "the" before them. For Example: Man is mortal – is the correct sentence.
Answer 5: Option C.

Explanation: Words like dozen, score, hundred, thousand, pair, million, etc. when preceded by a numeral are used as singulars. Another Example: I have four pair of shoes – is the correct sentence.

Answer 6: Option C.

Explanation: 'One of' or 'Any of' is always followed by plural verbs. Another Example: Any of these tools may serve my purpose – is the correct sentence.

Answer 7: Option A

Explanation: "For" is used in the Perfect Continuous Tense showing the approximate duration of action. They have been living in this house for six years – is the correct sentence.

Answer 8: Option C

Explanation: "Since" is used with the specific point of time and not approximation. Another Example: Since 2001, he has been living in Ludhiana – is the correct sentence.

Answer 9: Option E

Explanation: "Likely", "Certain", and "Sure" are always followed by "to". Another Example: We are sure to have help – is the correct sentence.

Answer 10: Option C

Explanation: "Lest" means "to avoid the risk of", "ऐसा न हो कि" Lest thus includes 'Not" in itself. Another Example: Walk fast lest you should miss the train – is the correct sentence.

Exercise 6

Adjectives: Adjectives are used almost exclusively to modify nouns, as well as any
phrase or part of speech functioning as a noun. For example:
• "John wears red glasses." (Red modifies the noun glasses.)
• "A loud group of students passed by." (Loud modifies the noun phrase group of students.)
• "Excellent writing is required for this job." (Excellent modifies the gerund writing.)
Attributive vs. Predicative

Adjectives: Adjectives are broken down into two basic syntactic categories: attributive

and predicative.

Adjectives that appear directly before (or sometimes directly after) the noun or pronoun they modify are known as attributive adjectives. These can appear anywhere in a sentence, and can modify parts of either the subject or the predicate.

Predicative adjectives, on the other hand, always appear after the noun they modify, connected to it by a linking verb. They are one of the three types of subject complements, and they are always part of the predicate —hence their name.

Let's compare two examples to highlight this difference:

• "The black dog is barking."

In this sentence, black is an <u>attributive adjective</u>. It is part of the noun phrase and is not connected to the noun dog by a linking verb. Now let's look at a predicative adjective:

• "The dog was black."

In this sentence, black is a <u>predicative adjective</u>. It follows dog, the noun that it modifies, and is connected to it by the linking verb was.

Modifying pronouns

While adjectives usually modify nouns, they can also modify pronouns.

This most commonly occurs when adjectives are predicative. For example:

• "That was great!"   • "She is very nice."   •   "A few were late."

Attributive adjectives can also modify indefinite pronouns, as in:

• "A happy few were able to attend the show."   •   "They were the lucky ones."

In informal speech or writing, it is not uncommon to modify personal pronouns attributively, as in:

• "Wow, lucky you!"   • "Silly me, I forgot to turn on the oven."

However, avoid using attributive adjectives with personal pronouns in anything other than casual conversation or writing.

Other categories of adjectives

Adjective Phrases and Clauses: In addition to the single-word adjectives we looked at above, we can also use adjective phrases and relative clauses (also called adjective clauses) to modify nouns.

Adjective Phrases: An adjective phrase is an adjective and any additional information linked to it that work together to describe a noun or pronoun in a sentence. This additional information can include determiners or adverbial modifiers. The adjective around which an adjective phrase is formed is known as the head word or head adjective of the phrase.

Adjective phrases can be either attributive (appearing before the nouns they

modify) or predicative (appearing after a linking verb)

For example:

- "You have a beautiful voice." (head word beautiful plus the determiner a)
- "He is a very good swimmer." (head word good plus the determiner a and the adverb very)
- "The helicopters are controlled remotely." (head word controlled plus the adverb remotely)
- "I am perfectly content on my own." (head word content plus the adverb perfectly and the adverbial prepositional phrase on my own)
- "They felt relieved to return home." (head word relieved plus the adverbial infinitive phrase to return home)

Note that prepositional phrases can also function as adjectives. These are considered adjectival phrases rather than true adjective phrases, because there is not a head adjective at the root of the phrase. Adjectival prepositional phrases always appear directly after the noun they modify.

For example:

- "The cat on the shed was old." (modifies the noun cat)
- "Please hand me that book over there." (modifies the noun book)

Relative Clauses (Adjective Clauses)

Relative clauses (also known as adjective or adjectival clauses) are dependent clauses that provide descriptive information about a noun or noun phrase. If the information it presents is essential to the meaning of the sentence, it is known as a restrictive clause; if it is extra information that is not essential, it is known as a non-restrictive clause. Relative clauses are introduced by either a relative pronoun or, less commonly, a relative adverb. Unlike attributive adjectives, they always appear directly after the noun they modify.

For example:

• "There's the woman who always sits next to me on the bus." (restrictive clause introduced by the relative pronoun who, modifying woman)

• "The book that I wrote is being published in January." (restrictive clause introduced by the relative pronoun that, modifying book)

• "The escaped giraffe, which had been on the loose for weeks, was finally captured." (non-restrictive clause introduced by the relative pronoun which, modifying giraffe)

• "The house where I was born is a very special place." (restrictive clause introduced by the relative pronoun where, modifying house)

• "I love casual Fridays, when we get to wear jeans to work." (nonrestrictive clause introduced by the relative adverb when, modifying casual Fridays)

Order of adjectives

We often use multiple adjectives to modify the same noun or pronoun. Note that these are not compound adjectives or adjective phrases, but rather individual adjectives that work independently to modify the same word. To avoid unnatural-sounding sentences when we use more than one adjective in this way, we put them in a specific order according to the type of description they provide. This is known as the order of adjectives:

1. Opinion (good, bad, strange, lovely)

2. Measurement (big, small, tiny, huge)

3. Shape (curved, straight, round, square)

4. Condition (wet, dry, clean, sad, happy)

5. Age (old, young, new, ancient)   6. Color (red, yellowish, transparent, blue)

7. Pattern (checked, striped, plaid, flowered)   8. Origin (American, British, eastern, western)

9. Material (wooden, plastic, steel, cloth)   10. Purpose (sleeping, shopping, work, gardening)

While we would almost never use a sentence with so many adjectives in a row, it's very common to use two or three. In this case, we generally must follow the order above, as in:

• "I bought an enormous rectangular Turkish rug on my vacation."
• "It is a long, heavy table."

In some circumstances we separate adjectives with commas and/or the coordinating conjunction and, while in other cases we use them without any separation at all.

Degrees of comparison

We can also use adjectives to create comparisons between two or more people or things, or to identify someone or something with the highest (or lowest) degree of some quality. To do this, we inflect (change the form of) the adjective to create comparative adjectives or superlative adjectives. For example:

• "I am strong." (basic adjective)
• "John is stronger than I am." (comparative adjective)
• "Janet is the strongest of us all." (superlative adjective)

This process of changing an adjective's form is known as the Degrees of Comparison.

Adjectives and Determiners

Adjectives and determiners both provide extra information about a noun (or pronoun). But while adjectives provide descriptive, modifying information about a noun, determiners are used to introduce and specify a noun.

The most common determiners are the articles the and a/an. These indicate whether a noun is specific or general (i.e., the book vs. a book).

Numbers can also act as determiners, as in three books, 10 books, 1000 books, etc.

Some other determiners are:

• demonstrative adjectives (this, that, these, those—also called demonstrative determiners);

• possessive adjectives (my, his, your, our—also called possessive determiners);

• interrogative adjectives (what, which, whose—also called interrogative determiners);

• distributive determiners (each, every, either—also called distributive adjectives;

• quantifiers (many, much, several, little).

Demonstratives and interrogatives are more commonly classed as adjectives, while possessives and distributives are more commonly classed as determiners; this is how they are grouped in this guide. Quantifiers are much harder to distinguish, but, for the purposes of this guide, they are covered in the chapter on Determiners.

Attributive Adjectives: Attributive adjectives are adjectives that describe a characteristic (or attribute) of the noun or pronoun that they modify. They form part of a noun phrase, appearing immediately before (or sometimes after) the noun in a sentence.

Attributive vs. Predicative

Adjectives: Attributive adjectives are usually considered in opposition to predicative adjectives, which follow the noun they modify and are connected to it by a linking verb. We can quickly illustrate the difference here:

• "The black dog is barking."

In this sentence, black is an attributive adjective. It is part of the noun phrase and is not connected to the noun dog by a linking verb. Now let's look at a predicative adjective:

• "The dog was black."

In this sentence, black follows the noun dog, the noun that it modifies, and is connected to it by the linking verb was; it is a predicative adjective.

While most adjectives can occur either as attributive adjectives or predicative adjectives, there are certain adjectives that can only occur predicatively. Most, but not all, of these adjectives begin with the letter "a":

Afloat afraid alike   alone   asleep awake   aware
Upset   well
For example:

✔ "The baby is asleep." (correct)

✘ "The asleep baby is in the crib." (incorrect)

✔ "The woman is well again." (correct)

✘ "The well woman got out of bed." (incorrect)

If you want to learn more about predicative adjectives, they are dealt with in greater detail in another section of this chapter.

Restrictive vs. Non-Restrictive: Attributive adjectives can be either restrictive or non-restrictive.
Restrictive adjectives help establish the identity of the noun or pronoun being modified, while non-restrictive adjectives simply help describe a noun that is already clearly identified. Note the difference between these two sentences:
• "She was emotional, and would avoid a sad film at all costs."
• "Titanic was a sad film that no viewer could finish with dry eyes."
In the first sentence, sad is restrictive: it tells us what kind of films she avoids. In the second sentence, sad is non-restrictive. We already know that Titanic is the film in question; the adjective sad simply serves to describe it further.

Prepositive adjectives (Before the noun): In simple sentences, attributive adjectives usually occur before the noun they modify, like in our first example, "The black dog is barking." Adjectives in this position are known as prepositive or prenominal adjectives. While most attributive adjectives can also occur as predicative adjectives after the noun, there are a number of specific adjectives which can only occur before the noun they modify. Some of these are: main, former, and mere.

✔ "The main idea is at the beginning of the paragraph." (correct)

✘ "The idea at the beginning of the paragraph is main." (incorrect)

Another adjective that only occurs attributively before the noun is the word utter, which provides heavy emphasis to the noun it modifies:

✔ "The dress was in utter ruin." (correct)

✘ "The ruin was utter." (incorrect)

Postpositive Adjectives: After the noun

It's fairly common to find attributive adjectives defined as "adjectives that are placed before the noun or pronoun they modify." However, it's a bit more complicated than that. While attributive adjectives are generally found before the noun they modify, especially in simple sentences, there are also many cases in which they are placed immediately after the noun.

When this happens, they are called postpositive or post-nominal adjectives. This often occurs in the following cases:

Terms derived from other languages

Postpositive adjective placement is very common in other languages, especially those derived from Latin. Postpositive placement in English occurs especially when using terms that were borrowed from French, a Latinderived language.

English borrows many official, military, governmental, and administrative terms from other languages, and the adjectives have retained their postpositive position. For example:

• Legal and financial terms: body politic, court-martial, pound sterling, accounts payable, and heir apparent.

• Important positions of individuals: secretary-general, poet laureate, attorney general, princess royal, and professor emeritus. In these types of terms, it's conventional to pluralize the noun, not the adjective. For example:

• "One poet laureate."   • "Two poets laureate."

However, it is becoming more and more common for writers to treat these terms as compound nouns, pluralizing the adjective instead of the noun:

• "Two poet laureates."

Traditional grammarians, though, consider the pluralization of the adjective to be incorrect.

After indefinite pronouns : Attributive adjectives almost always appear postpositively when they modify indefinite pronouns, such as someone, anyone, nobody, anyone, etc.

For example:

• "I wish I could find somebody perfect for the job."

• "We can give these jeans to anybody tall."

• "Is anyone talented at math here?"

After superlative attributive : Superlative adjectives are those that that compare three or more nouns to

indicate which exhibits the highest degree of something, for example: the best, the worst, the tallest, the biggest, etc. When a superlative adjective is used attributively before a noun, we can use other attributive adjectives in a postpositive position for emphasis.

• "Let's find the best hotel possible."

• "She's the worst singer present."

In addition, the attributive adjective can sometimes come before the noun when paired with a superlative, as in:

• "We climbed the highest nearby mountain."

Some adjectives ending in "-   able/-ible"

Often, attributive adjectives ending in "-able/-ible" are placed in the postpositive position:

• "It's the only time available."

• "It's the only option imaginable."

Be careful though, because sometimes placing an adjective of this type in the pre-positive or postpositive position can actually change the meaning of the sentence. For example:

• "She's looking for a responsible man."

In this sentence, responsible is in the pre-positive positive and seems to be a good characteristic. She is likely looking for a man who can be trusted. If we place the word responsible in the postpositive position, though, we have a very different meaning:

• "She's looking for the man responsible."

In this sentence, the word responsible takes on a different connotation, perhaps a negative one. She's looking for the man who has done something; in most cases, the "something" is negative, such as a mistake or even a crime. Not many adjectives change meaning so drastically based on their position in

the sentence, but it is something to be aware of.

After expressions of measurement

Nouns are often used in combination with numbers and adjectives to give measurements of height, depth, age, etc. For example:

• "He's only one year old."

• "She's five feet tall."

• "The river is five miles long."

• "The lake is one kilometer deep."

A notable exception to this pattern is when we discuss weight. Instead, we use the verb weigh and a unit of measurement, or else just the unit of weight after the verb be. For example:

✔ "She weighs 120 pounds." (correct)

✔ "She is 120 pounds." (correct)

✖ "She is 120 pounds heavy." (incorrect)

When the adjective modifies the object of factitive verbs

Factitive verbs are used to describe an action that results in a new condition or state of a person or thing. When an adjective modifies the direct object of a factitive verb, it is known as an object complement, and we place it in the postpositive position. For example:

- "He makes her happy."   • "I find horror films terrifying."
- "We painted the wall yellow."

For poetic effect: Postpositive placement of attributive adjectives is frequently used for poetic effect, as it gives a somewhat archaic and literary twist to otherwise plain expressions. Take for example this excerpt from the poem "Happiness," by Thomas Frederick Young:

"Fair Happiness, I've courted thee,   And used each cunning art and wile,

Which lovers use with maidens coy,   To win one tender glance or smile."

In this example, the poet places the adjectives coy after the plural noun maidens, instead of before it, creating a stronger poetic effect.

We can see the same effect again in the poem "The Bouquet," by Edward Smyth Jones:

"A blossom pink,   A blossom blue,

Make all there is in love   So true."

The same phenomenon can also be seen in titles of books and films, which often use postpositive placement for its dramatic effect. Consider the titles of works such as Jupiter Ascending, The Matrix Reloaded, or The Brothers Karamazov, for example.

Predicative Adjectives

Definition

A predicative adjective (or simply "predicate adjective") is used in the predicate of a clause to describe either the subject of the clause or the direct object of a verb.

As a subject complement

Predicative adjectives that describe the subject of the clause will follow a linking verb. In such cases, they are known as subject complements. For

example:

- "You look nice."   • "He is old."

Here, "nice" describes the subject "you," while "old" describes the subject "he."

Note that adjectives appearing immediately before the noun they are describing are known as attributive adjectives. For example: • "The old man seems nice."

"Old" is an attributive adjective that describes the subject, "man." "Nice" also describes "man," but it is a predicative adjective because it follows the linking verb "seems."

As an object complement: Predicative adjectives can also describe the direct object of non-linking verbs.

In this case, such adjectives function as object complements. For example: • "They painted the door red."

• "All that training made me stronger."

The predicative adjectives here are describing (complementing) the direct objects of the verbs, rather than the subjects of the sentences. "Red" describes the noun "door" (not the subject, "they"), while "stronger" describes the pronoun "me" (not the subject, "training").

Sense verbs: Certain verbs are used to indicate perceptions, opinions, or bodily sensations.

They are known as verbs of the senses, or "sense verbs" for short. Those verbs are as follows:

Taste   smell   sound

seem   feel   look   appear

Sense verbs merely relate the means by which the speaker has arrived at such a sensation about the subject. When we use them like this, they are functioning as linking verbs (rather than action verbs) and we pair them with predicative adjectives. This is not because the predicative adjective describes the verb, as an adverb would do. Rather, the predicative adjective describes the subject of the clause—they are subject complements, which we looked at above.

For example:

• "I feel terrible today." (A feeling inside of being very unwell.)

• "You sound tired." (A perception of tiredness in your voice.)

• "She didn't sound Italian." (An opinion based on the way her voice sounds.)

- "You look fabulous today." (This is my opinion when I look at you.)
- "He doesn't look very happy." (Again, my opinion based on what my eyes tell me. Note that the adverb "very" is modifying the adjective "happy," not the verb "look.")
- "This doesn't feel right." (An opinion or perception of something not being as it should.)
- "The car appears OK, but I'll have to drive it to be sure." (From what I can see, the car looks like it's in good condition.)
- "That smells nice." (Sensation of a pleasant aroma.)
- "This milk tastes funny*." (Sensation of an odd or unpleasant taste.)

*The adjective "funny" has two meanings. It can describe something that makes you laugh, or something that is strange, unpleasant, dubious, or not as it should be. It carries the latter meaning in the above example.

If any of the above verbs were used as action verbs, they could no longer be followed by an adjective—you would have to pair them with an adverb. For example:

- "I felt gently around the table in the dark." (Describes the action of feeling with one's hand.)
- "He looked quickly to the right." (Describes the action of looking in a certain direction.)
- "The car appeared out of nowhere." (Describes the action of coming into sight, using a prepositional phrase as an adverb.)
- "Yes, you heard right!" (Right in this case is an adverb meaning "accurately or correctly.")

Sources of confusion – Good vs. Well

A common stumbling block for natives and learners of English alike is the correct usage of good versus well.

In most instances, good is an attributive adjective directly describing a noun, while well is an adverb describing a verb, adjective, or other adverb. For

example:

- "He is a good driver."   - "She writes well."

We cannot use good and well interchangeably in these instances, and we can see immediately that the following would be incorrect:

✖ "He is a well driver."   ✖ "She writes good."

However, well can also function as a predicative adjective, where it usually means "healthy" or "not ill." We use it in this sense after linking verbs such as be, get, or the sense verbs above:

• "Jenny looks well lately."   • "Get well soon!"

In these examples, well does not describe the verbs, but rather the subjects of the sentences (implied in the second example).

Good can be used as a predicative adjective as well, meaning "of a high or satisfactory quality." This can be used after linking verbs to talk about an opinion of something, an emotional state, or general well-being (as opposed to physical health, specifically). For example:

• "The movie was good." (Opinion of the quality of the movie.)

• "I'm feeling good about my chances!" (Emotional state.)

• "Janet looks good lately." (Opinion of Janet's appearance.)

• A: "How are you, Bob?" B: "I'm good, thanks!" (General well-being.)

• Snehal is good in English. (Describing efficiency.)

The last example is perfectly correct, and it is very frequently used as a stock response to the question "How are you?" You could also say "I'm well," and no one is likely to take issue with it. However, if someone asks how you are after, for instance, an illness or injury, it would be better to respond with "I'm well."

If saying "I'm good" still does not sound quite right to you, you could also say "I am doing well," in which case well is used adverbially once more.

Proper Adjectives: Proper adjectives, like all adjectives, modify nouns, but they are different from other adjectives because they are actually formed from proper nouns. A noun, we know, is a person, place, or thing. We can distinguish between two types of nouns: common nouns and proper nouns. Common nouns are general, such as man, street, and city. James, Canning Street, and Paris are all proper nouns, because they talk about specific people, places, or things. "James" is a specific man, "Canning Street" is a specific street, and "Paris" is a specific city. Proper nouns are always written with a capital letter in English.

Proper adjectives are formed from these proper nouns, and they are also capitalized. They are often made from the names of cities, countries, or regions to describe where something comes from, but they can also be formed from the names of religions, brands, or even individuals. Some examples will make this clear: Proper Noun Proper Adjective Example Sentence

Italy Italian I love Italian food.

China Chinese How much does this Chinese robe cost?

Christ Christian In Europe, you can visit many ancient Christian churches.

Shakespeare Shakespearean He writes in an almost Shakespearean style.

Canon Canon I'm really excited to use my new Canon camera.

Why We Use Proper Adjectives

We use proper adjectives to describe something efficiently, directly, and explicitly. We could manage to avoid them, but it would result in clunky, awkward sentences. If we want to express the same meaning as the example sentences from the table above, we could write:

• "I love food that comes from Italy."

• "How much does this robe that comes from China cost?"

• "In Europe, you can visit many ancient churches of the religion that worships Christ."

• "He writes almost in the style of the writer Shakespeare."

• "I'm really excited to use my new camera from the Canon brand."

These sentences are lengthy, awkward, and choppy to read. Using the proper adjectives Italian, Chinese, Christian, Shakespearean, and Canon makes our meaning come across much more smoothly.

Proper adjectives are often used in an academic or artistic context, when the speaker (or writer) is addressing an audience of his or her peers and knows that they will quickly understand the reference. For example, the sentence "He writes in an almost Shakespearean style" would frequently be used among scholars of English literature. You would want to avoid the term Shakespearean if you were addressing a group of young students who had not yet heard of the author. Likewise, a group of architects or historians may refer to a "Romanesque building," while we would want to avoid that term if we were addressing a group that lacks background knowledge in historical architecture.

How to Form Proper Adjectives: A proper adjective is usually formed by adding an ending to the noun that it is derived from. There is not an easy rule to memorize for which ending to use. If you're not sure, you can try some of the most common endings—-ian, -an, -esque, -like, and -istic—and see which sounds right.

Proper Adjectives for Countries, Cities, and Regions
Many proper adjectives are formed from the names of countries to describe where a person, place, or thing is from. We have seen some examples already. The most common endings for nationalities are -ian/-ean/-an, -ic, ese, and -ish. The reason that English has so many endings for different nationalities is that we borrowed them from other languages. We borrowed the -ian, -ean, -an from Latin, -ic also from Latin but via Germanic languages, -ese from Italian, and -i from Arabic. The native Germanic suffix is -ish, which English has only kept for only a small number of nationalities. Here are some of the most common proper adjectives for countries: -ian/-ean/-an -ic -ese -i -ish -ish
Italian Greenlandic Chinese Iraqi Danish Chinese Armenian Icelandic Japanese Israeli Finnish Japanese
Australian Nordic Lebanese Pakistani Irish Lebanese Bulgarian Hispanic Portuguese Saudi Scottish Portuguese Korean Sudanese Emirati Spanish Sudanese Moroccan Vietnamese Yemeni Turkish Vietnamese
Proper adjectives can also describe what city or state/province something or someone comes from. Often, these are formed without an additional ending.
For example: "Let's have a New York bagel for breakfast."
• "She has a real London etiquette."
Other proper adjectives are formed by adding an ending to the name of the city or state, but it's impossible to learn them all. They're very irregular. You may find it useful to learn the endings for the most

famous cities of the world, or the places around where you live. Some examples of well-known proper adjectives for cities or states are:
• "I will never be able to keep up with Parisian fashion."
• "There is nothing better than Alaskan smoked salmon."
Regions
Finally, we also have proper adjectives for general geographic regions. For example:
• "An African elephant."   • "An Asian person."
• "A European museum."
• "A South American blanket."   • "A Middle Eastern film."
Sometimes, a word that began as a proper adjective can lose its "proper" significance over time. In these cases, the word is no longer capitalized. Take the following sentence:
• "He was making quixotic mistakes."
Quixotic was a proper adjective derived from the name Don Quixote, a fictional character who was prone to foolish, grandiose behavior. Through time, it has come to mean "foolish" in its own right, without necessarily pointing to the character of Don Quixote. Therefore, it has lost its capitalization.
Another example of this phenomenon is the word gargantuan. Once associated with the name of a giant in a 16th-century book, it has come to mean "huge" in daily use. Since losing its link with the fictional monster, it is no longer capitalized.
• "The couple purchased the house next door and built a gargantuan house."
On the other hand, there are some common nouns that can act as proper nouns in specific cases and need to be capitalized. For example, the adjective native would normally be considered a common noun, as in the sentence "I want to practice Spanish with a native speaker." Consider the word native in
the following sentence, though:
• The indigenous people of Canada and the United States are commonly referred to as Native Americans. In this sentence, Native acts as a proper adjective because it describes a specific group of people, just like

Italian or French. When a proper adjective needs a prefix, make sure to place a hyphen
between the prefix and the proper adjective. Don't capitalize the prefix, though. For example:

• "He was accused of stirring up anti-Chinese sentiment."
• "I love studying pre-Shakespearean theater."

The exception to this rule is if the prefix is formed from a proper noun itself, as in the "Austro-Hungarian empire." In this example, both Hungarian and its prefix Austro are derived from proper nouns (Hungary and Austria), so they are both capitalized.

Lastly, while proper adjectives are generally placed before the noun they modify, most can also be placed after the noun, provided that there is also a linking verb before them. For example, all of the following sentences are correct:

• "The winning team was Spanish.　　• "The man over there is Italian."

• "The monks in this monastery are Buddhist."

Quiz 001

1. Which of the following parts of speech are adjectives not able to modify?

a) Nouns　　　　b) Pronouns　　c) Adverbs　　　d) B & C

2. Adjectives that appear after linking verbs are known as:

a) Attributive adjectives　　　　b) Predicative adjectives

c) Demonstrative adjectives　　　d) Interrogative adjectives

3. Which of the following types of adjectives are formed from two or more words and a hyphen?

a) Compound adjectives　　　　b) Nominal adjectives

c) Proper adjectives　　　　　　d) Collective adjectives

4. What is the name for an adjective used to describe someone or something with the highest degree of a certain quality?

a) Comparable adjectives　　　　b) Comparative adjectives

c) Superior adjectives　　　　　 d) Superlative adjectives

5. Which of the following often have properties similar to adjectives?

a) Adverbs　　　b) Particles　　　c) Determiners　d) Conjunctions

Quiz 002

1. Which of the following is an example of an attributive adjective?

a) A black dog.   b) The dog is black.

c) The dog black.   d) The dog.

2. Which of the following is not an attributive adjective?

a) Sarah is short.   b) The blond girl went to the party.

c) My dear friend James is here.   d) Have you called your poor brother?

3. Attributive adjectives never _____.

a) come after the noun.   b) precede the noun.

c) follow a linking verb.   d) appear in the postpositive position.

4. Most adjectives that are never attributive begin with the letter "_____."

a) A   b) B   a) C   b) D

5. Which sentence is traditionally considered to be more correct?

a) The secretary-generals of the three countries are meeting today.

b) The secretaries-general of the three countries are meeting today.

Quiz 003

1. What is the function of an adjective when it describes a noun that is part of the predicate?

a) Subject complement   b) Object complement

c) Attributive adjective   d) None of the above

2. What does a predicative adjective that follows a linking verb modify?

a) The verb   b) The object of the verb

c) The subject of the clause   d) The predicate of the clause

3. When can "well" function as a predicative adjective? (Choose the answer that is most correct.)

a) When it follows a linking verb b) When it modifies a linking verb

c) When it means "in good health"   d) When it functions as an object complement

e) A & C   f) B & D

4. Which of the following sentences does not have a predicate adjective?

a) "I don't think I heard you right."   b) "I am feeling well."
c) "My father is really nice."   d) "Does this seem different to you?"

Quiz 004

1. Which of the following is a proper adjective?

a) Blue   b) Spanish   c) Tall   d) Tired

2. Which of the following is not a proper adjective?

a) Spanish   b) Grecian   c) Intelligent   d) Muslim

3. In the sentence "I went to a private catholic school," which word or words should be capitalized?

a) catholic   b) private c) school   d) catholic and school

4. In the sentence "The number of afro-europeans has risen steadily," which word or words should be capitalized?

a) number   b) afro c) Europeans   d) afro and europeans

5. Proper adjectives are adjectives formed from _____.

a) proper nouns   b) common nouns c) adjectives d) verbs

Answer Key:

001. Adjectives: 1-c, 2-b, 3-a, 4-d, 5-c
002. Attributive Adjectives: 1-a, 2-a, 3-c, 4-a, 5-b
003. Predicative Adjectives: 1-b, 2-c, 3-e, 4-a
004. Proper Adjectives: 1-b, 2-c, 3-a, 4-d, 5-a

Exercise 7

Question 1.

Read the conversation given below and complete the paragraph that follows: (3 marks) (Board 2014, Set PRE2N18)

Principal: Why were you absent last week?

Student: I was absent because I was not well.

Principal: What will happen to your studies now?

Student: I will work hard to complete them.

The Principal asked the student (a)………… The student replied (b)…………… The Principal was concerned and asked (c)………… The student replied that he would study hard to complete them.

Answer:

(a) why he had been absent the previous week.

(b) that he had been absent because he had not been well.

(c) what would happen to his studies then?

You can master in English Grammar of various classes by our articles like Tenses, Clauses, Prepositions, Story writing, Unseen Passage, Notice Writing, etc.

Question 2.

Read the conversations given below. Based on your reading, fill in the blanks appropriately. (3 marks) (Board Term-1 2013, Set 8SRR)

Julie: When is the fancy- dress competition in your school?

Mona: It is after two weeks.

Julie: Are you taking part in it?

Mona: Yes, I am taking part as an engine driver.

Julie: Why have you chosen that?

Mona: So that I can reach late.

Julie asked Mona when the fancy dress competition in her school was. To that

Mona replied that (a) _____________ Julie enquired whether (b) _____________ Mona said that she was taking part as an engine driver. Julie asked why (c) _____________ She answered (d) _____________.

Answer:

(a) it was after two weeks.

(b) whether/if she was taking part in it.

(c) she had chosen that.

(d) then/so that she could reach late.

Question 3.

Read the conversation given below and complete the paragraph that follows : (3 marks) (Board Term-1 2013, Set 5007)

Haiku: The landlord has come. Take out the money you have set aside.

Wife: But there are only three' hundred rupees. If you give them to him, where is the blanket going to come from?

Haiku: Don't worry. I will figure out some other plan.

Haiku told his wife that the landlord had come, she should take out (a) …………… His wife said that (b)…………and asked him if he gave them to him (c)…………..

Answer:

(a) the money she had set aside.

(b) that there were only three hundred rupees.

(c) where the blanket was going to come from.

Question 4.

Read the conversation given below and complete the passage that follows : (3 marks) (Board Term-1 2012, Set EC2,039)

Ali: Omar, why don't you leave this place? I can drop you on my way back home.

Omar: I have no home.

Ali: Where have you come from?

Omar: From Tunisia.

Ali asked Omar (a)………………..and offered to (b)……………….. Omar replied that he had no home. Then Ali asked (c)……………….. Omar told him that he had come from Tunisia.

Answer:

(a) why he didn't leave that place.

(b) drop him on his way back home.

(c) where he had come from.

Question 5.

Read the following conversation between a mother and son and then complete the paragraph that follows : (3 marks) (Board Term-1 2012, Set EC2,043)

Mother: You seem so tired. Take some rest.

Suraj: I can't even think of relaxing. I have lots of homework to do.

Mother: You should not take so much of stress.

Suraj: Don't worry. Please give me a hot cup of tea.

Mother said to Suraj that (a)…………………… Suraj replied that (b)………………… The mother advised him not to take so much of stress. Suraj told his mother (c)…………………

Answer:

(a) he seemed so tired and advised him to take a rest.

(b) he could not even think of relaxing as he had lots of homework to do.

(c) not to worry and requested her to give him a hot cup of tea.

Question 6.

Given below are instructions for making soup. Use these to complete the blanks in the paragraph that follows. (3 marks) (Board Tenn-I 2012, Set EC2,042)

Mix the soup powder with 750 ml of water without allowing it to form lumps.

Pour the mixture into a heavy-bottomed vessel.

Bring it to a boil, stirring continuously.

Simmer the soup for five minutes.

Pour the soup into soup bowls and serve garnished with fried croutons.

The packet containing the soup powder (a) _____________ opened and the contents are mixed with 750 ml of water without allowing it to form lumps. The mixture (b) _____________ into a heavy-bottomed vessel. It is stirred continuously and brought to boil. The soup (c) _____________ on a slow flame for five minutes. Finally after the soup is ready, it is (d) _____________.

Answer:

(a) is opened

(b) is poured

(c) is simmered

(d) is poured into the soup bowls and served

Question 7.

Read the conversation given below and complete the paragraph that follows: (3 marks) (Board Term-1 2012, Set EC2,0401)

Raju: Do you know Varun was hit by a two-wheeler yesterday?

Arun: Oh no! When did it happen?

Raju: He was hit by a scooter on his way back from school.

Arun: Is he badly hurt?

Raju asked Arun (a)....................... Arun was shocked and wanted to know when (b)....................... Raju replied that (c)....................... Arun enquired if he was badly hurt.

Answer: (a) if he knew that Varun had been hit by a two-wheeler the previous day.

(b) it had happened. .

(c) he had been hit by a scooter on his way back from school.

Question 8.

Read the conversation given below and complete the paragraph that follows: (3 marks) (Board Term-1 2012, Set EC2,064)

Vani: Harika, are you going to join the Dramatics Club with me?

Harika: No, I am going to join the Adventure Club.

Vani: I too would have joined the Adventure Club, but I am very scared of heights.

Harika: If that is the case, join the Dramatics Club.

Vani asked Harika (a)…………………….. Harika said that (b)………………….… Adventure Club. To this Vani replied (c) ………………….… Adventure Club, but she was very scared of heights. Harika advised her to join the Dramatics Club.

Answer:

(a) if she was going to join the Dramatics Club with her.

(b) she was going to join the

(c) she too would have joined the

Question 9.

Read the conversation given below and complete the paragraph that follows: (Board Term-1 2012, Set EC2,039)

Pig: See how strong and hefty I am. Even the Jumbo was afraid of me.

Animals: Jumbo, was it out of horror?

Jumbo: I could have happily crushed the dirty pig under my heels but I avoided it so that I do not become dirty.

The jaunty pig said (a)……………………….. He further added (b)……………………….. All the animals enquired of Jumbo if that had been out of horror. Jumbo replied that he could have happily crushed the dirty pig under his heels but he (c)………………………..

Answer:

(a) that he was very strong and hefty

(b) that even the Jumbo had been afraid of him.

(c) had avoided it so that he did not become dirty.

Question 10.

Read the conversation given below and complete the paragraph that follows: (3 marks)

Rohan: When is the fancy dress competition at your school?

Seema: It is after two weeks.

Rohan: Are you taking part in it?

Seema: Yes, I am taking part as a caterpillar.

Rohan: Why have you chosen that?

Seema: So that I can reach late.

Rohan asked Seema (a)........................... Seema replied (b).......................... Rohan enquired (c)....................... Seema said that she was taking part as a caterpillar. Rohan asked why she had chosen that. Seema answered so that she could reach late. (Board Term-12012, Set EC2,048)

Answer:

(a) when the fancy dress competition in her school was.

(b) that it was after two weeks.

(c) whether she was taking part in that

Question 11.

Read the conversation given below and complete the paragraph that follows : (3 marks) (Board Term-1 2012, Set EC2,061)

Customer: Why is the meal so sour?

Waiter: Nobody has complained for five days sir, about the meal.

Customer: What! Where is the Manager?

Waiter: He has gone to some other hotel to take dinner, sir.

One day a customer was taking dinner in a hotel. He asked the waiter why (a)........................... The waiter told him (b) .... At this, the customer was shocked and wanted to know where the Manager was. The waiter replied (c) ....

Answer:

(a) the meal was so sour.

(b) that nobody had complained for five days about the meal.

(c) that he had gone to some other hotel to take dinner.

Question 12.

Read the conversation given below and complete the paragraph that follows : (3 marks) (Board Term-1 2012, Set EC2,049)

Teacher: Did you brush your hair this morning?

Asha: Yes, I did, but the wind blew it about while I was coming to school.

Teacher: Wear a hairband tomorrow.

The teacher asked Asha (a)…………………….. Asha replied that she had, but the wind (b)……………………while she had been coming to school. The teacher instructed her (c)………………………

Answer:

(a) if she had brushed her hair that morning.

(b) had blown it about.

(c) to wear a hairband the next day.

Question 13.

Read the following conversation and complete the paragraph that follows : (3 marks)

Mother: Rita, finish your food.

Rita: I don't want to have this food. You never give me a pizza or burger.

Mother: They are not good for health. You had pizza at your friend's birthday party last evening.

Rita: OK, then give me French fries and shake. '

Mother: If you live only on junk food, you will spoil your health.

Mother told Rita (a)……………………….. Rita replied that (b)……………………….and told her mother that she never gave her a pizza or burger. Mother said that they were not good for health and reminded her (c)…………………… Rita then asked her mother to give her french fries and a shake. Mother warned her that if she lived only on junk food, she would spoil her health.

Answer:

(a) to finish her food.

(b) she did not want to have that food

(c) that she had pizza at her friend's birthday party the evening before.

Question 14.

Read the conversation/dialogue given below and complete the paragraph that follows: (3 marks)

Patient: I want an appointment with the doctor for this evening.
Receptionist: I'm sorry, I can't give you an appointment before the 20th.
Patient: But I could be dead by then!
Receptionist: That's all right. I'll ring up your wife and cancel the appointment in that case.
The patient (a)………………….evening. The receptionist (b)………………….an appointment before the 20th. The patient (c)…………………… The receptionist replied that it was all right as she would ring up his wife and cancel the appointment in that case.
Answer:
told the receptionist that he wanted an appointment with the doctor for that
(b) replied that she was sorry but she could not give him
(c) exclaimed that he could be dead by then
Question 15.
Read the conversation given below and complete the paragraph that follows: (3 marks)
Patient: Good afternoon. I need to get an E.C.G. done. .
Receptionist: Sorry. Our machine is not working. You can come tomorrow.
Patient: What! But I think I'm having a heart attack now.
Receptionist: Oh! In that case, 1 will book you for a bypass and inform our Senior Cardiologist.
A patient went to the doctor's clinic, greeted the receptionist, and said that (a)……………………… The receptionist apologized and told him (b) ……………………… She also added that (c) ………………………. The patient reacted angrily and said he thought he was having a heart attack. To this, the receptionist replied that in that case she could book him for a bypass and inform their Senior Cardiologist.
Answer:
(a) he needed to get an E.C.G. done.
(b) that their machine was not working.
(c) he could come the next day.
2. Process Writing (3 marks each)

Question 1.

Given below are instructions on how to make cold coffee. Refer to the given notes and complete the paragraph : (3 marks) (Board Term-12012, Set EC2,046)

Pour 3/4 of a glass of cold milk in the mixer.

Add one teaspoonful of sugar and half a teaspoonful coffee powder to it.

Add a few ice cubes.

Switch on the mixer.

Coffee and sugar would blend with the milk and froth would appear on top.

Switch off the mixer.

Pour cold coffee in a tall glass.

Serve it cold.

To prepare cold coffee 3/4 of a glass of cold milk (a)..................... One teaspoonful of sugar and half a teaspoonful of coffee powder (b).....................to it. A few ice cubes are also added to this. The mixer (c)..................... When froth appears on the milk, the mixer is switched off. After pouring it in a tall glass it is served cold.

Answer:

(a) is taken

(b) are added

(c) is switched on

Question 2.

Given below are the instructions on How to Make Orange Squash. Refer, to the notes and complete the paragraph given below: (3 marks)

Take 1 dozen fully ripe oranges

Remove the rind

Extract the juice

Strain through a thick cloth

Mix 1 /2 kg sugar, 1 /2 tea-spoonful citric acid

Add a pinch of potassium meta-bisulfate, a few drops of colour and essence

Stir till thoroughly dissolved

One dozen fully ripe oranges are taken. Their rinds (a)....................and the juice (b)..................... Then the juice (c)...................through a thick cloth into a stainless steel vessel. 1/2 kg of sugar, 1/2 teaspoonful of citric acid, a pinch of potassium meta – bisulphate, a few drops of colour and essence are added to the juice. The mixture is stirred till it is thoroughly dissolved.

Answer:

(a) are removed

(b) is extracted

(c) is strained

Question 3.

Given below are a set of instructions for using a clinical thermometer. Complete the paragraph describing the process of using a clinical thermometer: (3 marks) (Board Term-1 2012, Set EC2,052)

Wash the thermometer with fresh water thoroughly.

Stake it well to bring down the reading below 37°C.

Place the die bulb of the thermometer under the patient's tongue.

Ask the patient to keep the mouth closed.

Keep the thermometer under the patient's tongue for at least 2 minutes.

Take out the thermometer and read the temperature.

How to Use a Clinical Thermometer

The clinical thermometer (a)....................with freshwater and the reading (b)....................by shaking it well. Then the bulb of the thermometer (c)....................under the patient's tongue and he is asked to keep the mouth closed. The thermometer should be kept there for at least two minutes. It is then taken out and the temperature is read.

Answer:

(a) is washed   (b)) is brought down   (c) is placed

Question 4.

Given below are instructions on how to make lemonade. Refer to the notes and complete the paragraph: (3 marks) (Board Term-1 2012, Set EC2,048)

Take a glass of water.

Add four spoonfuls of sugar.

Squeeze the juice of a lemon and add.

Add salt, roasted cumin seed powder, and ice.

Serve chilled.

To prepare lemonade, a glass of water is taken and four spoonfuls of sugar (a)....................to it. A lemon (b)....................and juice is added to it. Salt, roasted cumin seed powder and ice (c).................... It is served chilled.

Answer:

(a) are added

(b) is squeezed

(c) are added and stirred

Question 5.

Given below are instructions on how to make instant coffee. Refer to the given notes and complete the paragraph: (3 marks) (Board Term-1 2012, Set EC2,083)

Put coffee powder and sugar into a cup – pour some hot milk – stir it well for 5 minutes – add hot milk to it – Add a pinch of cinnamon powder for flavour – serve hot.

To prepare instant coffee, coffee powder, and sugar

(a)....................in a cup. Some hot water

(b)....................into the cup and the mixture is

(c)....................for about 5 minutes. Hot milk is then added to it.

It is then served hot with cinnamon powder for taste.

Answer: (a) is put   (b) is poured   (c) stirred

Question 6.

Given below are instructions to make tomato soup. Read the given notes and complete the paragraph that follows: (3 marks) (Board Term-12012, Set EC2,018)

Place tomatoes in a pan-fill the pan with water–add onions and green chilies –cook for 10 min.-remove from the pan–peel tomatoes–grind tomatoes, onion, green chilies–add salt to taste–boil and serve hot.

To prepare tomato soup tomatoes (a)....................in a pan and the pan is filled with water. Onions and green chilies

(b)....................and cooked for 10 minutes. Tomatoes are then

(c)....................and peeled. Tomatoes, onions, and chilies are ground. After adding salt the mixture is boiled and served hot.

Answer: (a) are placed (b) are added

(c) removed from the pan

Question 7.

Given below are the instructions on dyeing a piece of cloth. Refer to the given notes and complete the , sentences given below: (3 marks) (Board Term-1 2012, Set EC2,039)

Take a strong, white-coloured cotton cloth.

Boil water and add the desired colour.

Dip the cloth in coloured hot water and soak it for half an hour.

Take the cloth out

Spread the cloth and let it dry.

A strong, white-coloured cotton cloth is taken. Water

(a).....................and the desired colour (b)...................... The

cloth (c)....................in the coloured water for half an hour. The

cloth is taken out. Finally, it is spread and allowed to dry.

Answer:

(a) is boiled (b) is added to it   (c) is soaked

Question 8.

Given below are the instructions on how to use a thesaurus. Refer to the given notes and complete the paragraph: (3 marks) (Board Term-1 2012, Set EC2,061)

Locate the word for which you need synonyms in the Thesaurus.

Note the number given after that word.

Look up the alternatives listed against that number.

Choose the one that best suits the purpose.

First, the word for which (a)....................in the Thesaurus. Next, the

number given is noted. After these alternatives listed

(b)..................... Finally, the one best (c).....................

Answer:

(a) synonyms are needed is located

(b) are looked up against the number

(c) that suits the purpose is chosen

Question 9.

Read the instructions given below and complete the following: (3 marks) (Board Term-12012, Set EC2,053)

Don't leave valuables inside your vehicle.

Don't display large sums of cash in public.

Don't touch any unidentified object.

Don't get distracted by unknown persons trying to approach you with any offer of help.

Make your city safe and sound by following certain instructions. No valuables (a)....................inside a vehicle as they may attract anti-social elements. While carrying cash it (b)...................... If we find some unidentified object lying in the market it (c)..................... We should not get distracted by unknown persons trying to approach us with an offer to help.

Answer: (a) should be left   (b) should not be displayed in public (c) should not be touched

Question 10.

Given below are the instructions on how to make coconut burfi. Refer to the given notes and complete the paragraph: (3 marks) (Board Term-I 2012, Set EC2,059)

Stir together grated coconut mid condensed milk — cook on high in the microwave for 7 mins — switching off, opening and stirring every 30 seconds — add the almonds and cardamom in the hot and bubbling coconut mixture-pour the mixture into the prepared pan.

To prepare 'coconut burfi' grated coconut and condensed milk are stirred together in a large microwave-safe bowl. Then, it (a)...................on high in the microwave for 7 minutes. It (b)..................., opened, and stirred every 30 seconds.

When the coconut mixture is hot and bubbling, almonds, and cardamom (c)..................... The mixture is poured into a prepared pan and after cooling, cut into small squares with a greased knife.

Arts.   (a) is cooked   (b) is switched off   (c) are added

Question 11.

Some steps for an experiment to prove that unlike charges attract each other. Complete the paragraph given below, using suitable words. (3 marks) (Board Term-I 2011, Set 42)

Take a hard rubber rod and a piece of flannel.

Electrify the rod by rubbing it with flannel.

Suspend the rod with a silk thread.

Electrify a glass rod by rubbing it with a silk cloth.

Bring the glass rod near the suspended rubber rod.

The glass rod would attract the rubber rod.

First of all, a hard rubber rod and a piece of flannel are taken. The rod is, then (a)…………. A glass rod is, then, (b)……………….. by rubbing it with a silk cloth. The glass rod (c)……………….. near the suspended rubber rod. The rubber rod will be attracted by the glass rod.

Answer:

(a) electrified   (b) again electrified   (c) is then brought

Question 12.

Using the information given below, complete the paragraph that follows. The fust one has been done as an example. Don't write the printed words. (3 marks) (Board Term-I 2011, Set 29)

Cut a fresh onion into small pieces.

(ii) Boil these pieces in 10 ml of distilled water for 3-4 min.

(iii) Coal the solution.

(iv) Filter the content to be used as food extract.

(v) Perform Benedict's test.

(vi) The solution turns green, then orange, and finally red.

(vii) This confirms the presence of glucose in onion.

In order to test the presence of glucose in onions, the following experiment must be performed. First, the onion is cut into small pieces. Then these onion pieces (a)……………….. for 3-4 minutes. The solution is allowed to cool. It is then (b)………………… Now (c)……………….. on the content. You will observe that initially, the solution turns green, then orange, and finally red. Thus, the presence of glucose in onion is confirmed.

Answer:

(a) are boiled in 10 ml of distilled water.

(b) filtered to be used as food extract.

(c) Benedict's test is performed.

Question 13.

Given below are instructions for making soup. Refer to the given notes and complete the paragraph that follows: (3 marks)

Mix the soup powder with 750 ml, of water without allowing it to form lumps.

Pour the mixture into a heavy-bottomed vessel.

Bring it to boil, stirring continuously.

Let the soup simmer for five minutes.

Pour the soup into soup bowls and serve garnished with fried croutons.

The packet containing soup powder is opened and the contents are mixed with 750 ml of water without allowing it to form lumps. The mixture (a)....................into a heavy-bottomed vessel. It is stirred (b)....................boil. The soup (c)....................on a slow flame for five minutes. Finally, after the soup is ready, it is served garnished with fried croutons.

Answer: (a) is poured   (b) and brought to boil
(c) is allowed to simmer
3. News Headlines (3 marks each)
Question 1. Read the newspaper headlines given below. Complete the sentences that follow: (3 marks) (Board Term-1 2014, Set EC2,049)
70% INFANT DEATHS IN-FIRST 29 DAYS
Nearly 70% of infant deaths in the country in the year 2010......................during the first 29 days of the infant's life.
(b) PARKING ROW: MAN BATTERED TO DEATH
A 45-year-old autorickshaw driver.......................to death over a parking issue in Geeta Colony on Sunday.
(c) MINOR POLIO VICTIM HURT IN HOSPITAL
17-year-old polio afflicted girl ....inside a government hospital.
Answer: (a) took place (b) was beaten (c) was hurt
Question 2.
Read the news items given below. Use the information in the headlines to complete the sentences that follow: (3 marks) (Board Term-1 2012, Set EC2,058)

Govt, raises DA; announcement made
The government.......................for its employees with effect from 1st July 2012
(b) Kalka Shatabdi cancelled due to heavy rains
The heavy rains caused flooding of the railway tracks because of which Kalka Shatabdi
(c) Petrol, diesel prices likely to be raised
The government.......................the prices of petrol and diesel to ensure that the public sector oil companies do not face losses
Answer:
(a) has announced a raise in DA   (b) has been cancelled
(c) is considering raising

Question 3. Read the newspaper headlines given below and complete the news items: (3 marks) (Board Term-1 2012, Set EC2,038)
NEGLECT CAUSED MALL TRAGEDY, SAYS PROBE
The tragedy at The Great Adventure Mall…………………..due to neglect on the part of authorities.
(b) FOUR HURT AS CYLINDER BLAST TRIGGERS COLLAPSE
Four members of a family including two children………………….when portions of their first-floor house collapsed following a gas cylinder explosion in Delhi's Nand Nagri on Sunday morning.
(c) TWO AUTO – LIFTERS NABBED, POLICE CRACK 30 CASES
The South District Police claims to have …………………..the arrest of two persons on Sunday.
Answer: (a) was caused   (b) were injured
(c) cracked 30 cases of auto-lifting with
Question 4. Read the given headlines and complete the reports that follow: (3 marks) (Board Term-1 2012, Set EC2,034)
CHIEF SEEKS MORE TIME FROM CBI
NEW DELHI: Army chief General VK Singh…………………..the CBI for more time to provide details on his allegation that he was offered ?Rs.14 crore bribe.
(b) Rs.1 CR TO THE WIFE OF ACCIDENT VICTIM
The Delhi High Court…………………..a compensation of ? 1 crore to the widow of a businessman who died in a road accident five years ago.
(c) DEATH PENALTY TO THREE FOR KILLING GIRL OVER PROPERTY
NEW DELHI: A man, along with his daughter and son…………………..death penalty by a Delhi court for burning alive his daughter-in-law to comer her property.
Answer:
(a) has asked   (b) has awarded (c) have been given
Question 5. Read the heading given below and complete the news stories : (3 marks)
Pawar, Daughter Deny Involvement In IPL
Sharad Pawar and his daughter Supriya Sule on

Friday...........cricket team.

(b) IM Declared Terror Outfit

The Indian Mujahideen (IM), suspected to be a shadow outfit of the banned Students' Islamic Movement of India..................a terror outfit.

(c) 5 Passengers Killed as Train Rams into Mini-Bus

............at an unmanned level crossing on Friday when a train rammed into a mini-bus.

Answer:

(a) denied having any involvement in any Indian Premier League (b) has been declared (c) Five persons were killed

Question 6.

Read the news items given below. Use the information in the headlines to complete the sentences. Write the answer in your answer sheet against the correct blank numbers. Do not copy the whole sentences: (3 marks) (Board Term-1 2011, Set 16)

Stone chamber of 3rd-century tomb unveiled

A third-century stone chamber....................by Japanese archaeologists today. It was excavated from an ancient tomb in Nara.

(b) Abducted Bengal cop released by Maoists.

Two days after being taken hostage, police officer A.

Dutt....................unharmed by the Maoists in Lalgarh.

(c) Singaporean trade team to visit India.

According to the Singapore Chamber of Commerce, a high-level trade team................. India soon to finalize the setting up of the trade development council in New Delhi.

Answer: (a) has been unveiled   (b) has been released

(c) will be visiting/is going to visit

.

Exercise 8

Ex. 1. Find the passive verbs in this text. What tenses are they?

In Denmark, 24 people were left hanging upside down when a roller coaster car made an unscheduled stop.

The passengers were stranded 60 feet in the air for 20 minutes before firemen arrived with ladders.
An official for the fairground, at Alborg in Western Denmark, said the riders had been firmly locked in and not been in danger.
"They were given their money back", the official said.

Ex. 2. Underline all the passives.

Acid rain is caused by burning coal and oil. When either fuel is burned, it releases poisonous gases which are carried up into the atmosphere and sometimes transported long distances.

Over 3000 research projects have been carried out to look into acid rain, and a decision to tackle the problem has been taken in most of the western European countries. Measures have been taken in Scandinavia and in Central Europe to stop the pollution before it is dumped on the environment: and a diplomatic campaign has been launched to countries that the problem has to be considered as a major ecological threat.

"Five years ago this issue was not being treated seriously," says one of the leading environmental group, "but now that damage has been reported in large areas of forest and Lakeland our politicians are being forced to take action. This problem must be solved quickly: if governments do nothing, they will be faced in two or three years time with the accusation that they have allowed our forests to die." A major international initiative to combat acid rain is expected in the near future.

Note that the rules for choice of tense are the same in the passive as they are in the active sentences.

Ex. 3. Put the sentences into the Passive voice.

    1. We hear a sound of a violin in the hall.

2. His father always praises him when he works hard.
3. My sister often takes Bob for his brother.
4. My mother wakens me at 7 o'clock every morning.
5. We use this room for special occasions.
6. In some districts farmers use pigs to find truffles.
7. They make these artificial flowers of silk.
8. They feed the seals at the zoo twice a day.
9. Beavers make these dams.
10. They sell soft drinks here.
11. Most people oppose such things.
12. Usually students do a lot of work in spring.
13. They don't admit children under sixteen.
14. Now they start these engines by electricity.
15. They never discuss it in her presence.

Ex.4. Put the sentences into the Passive voice.

1. She found the envelope at last behind the dining-room clock.
2. I bought this book a weak ago a week ago.
3. A great artist painted this picture.
4. John broke the window the other day
5. The mob broke all the shop windows in recent riots.
6. They rang the church bells as a flood warning.
7. It is high time someone told him to stop behaving like a child.
8. The judge gave him two weeks in which to pay the fine.
9. An uneasy silence succeeded the shot.
10. They showed her the easiest way to do it.
11. Lightning struck the old oak.
12. A jelly-fish stung her.
13. Did the idea interest you?
14. They used to start these engines by hand.
15. Who wrote it?

Ex. 5. Put the sentences into the Passive voice.

1. I shall post this letter tomorrow.
2. They will discuss your report next week.
3. The secretary will change our time-table in a week.
4. Tom will meet us at station.
5. Someone will serve refreshments.
6. The lawyer will give him the details of his uncle's will.

7. The closure of the workshops will make a lot of people redundant.
8. We will not admit children under sixteen.
9. She will wear an evening dress.
10. The organisers will exhibit the paintings till the end of the month.
11. They will say nothing more about the matter.
12. The police will interview him tomorrow.
13. We shall discuss this problem later.
14. What measures shall we take?
15. I shall send him this report tomorrow.

Ex 6. Mixed Tenses. Put the sentences into the Passive.

1)   a) They told me an interesting story yesterday.

b) They offered him a cup of tea.

c) They promised us a interesting book.

d) They pay him regularly.

e) They will show us some new magazines.

f) They teach the children French and German.

g) They gave him an invitation card to the party.

h) They granted him the film a long term credit.

2) Fire almost completely <u>destroyed</u> the Royal Hotel last night. By the time someone <u>called</u> the Fire Brigade, the hotel was already blazing. Ambulance <u>took</u> fifteen people to hospital suffering from severe burns. They <u>say</u> that seven of them are in a serious condition. People <u>think</u> that a discarded cigarette <u>started</u> the fire.

(E.g.: The Royal Hotel was almost completely destroyed by fire last night By the time the Fire Brigade was/were called, ...)

3) Last month the Council <u>put forward</u> a plan to make the seafront traffic free. Many of the shop and restaurant owners <u>support</u> the plan as they believe that a more pleasant environment <u>will improve</u> their trade. However, the hotel owners are less enthusiastic and say that the traffic restriction <u>will make</u> access to their car parks very difficult. There have also been protects from local residents who complain that the closure of the seafront road <u>will make</u> their journeys around the town much longer.

Ex. 7. Open the brackets.

1. My car (damage) last night.
2. This computer (make) in the USA.
3. The machine (make) in Scotland.
4. The President (kill) last night.
5. The money (change into dollars) at the bank.
6. The parcel (post) yesterday.
7. Cheese (make) from milk.
8. The children (give) some food.
9. The house (paint) every ear.
10. Several people (hurt) in an accident last night.
11. He (show) the way to the station.
12. She (tell) the news when she returned home.
13. They (offer) the goods at a low price.
14. Children (teach) foreign languages at school.
15. They (pay) twice a month.
16. He (offer) some interesting work..
17. He (promise) immediate help.
18. The buyers (grant) a credit of six months.
19. They (give) detailed directions tomorrow.
20. The film (show) to us at 6 o'clock.
21. The child hopes he (give) a computer by Santa Claus, but his parents made up their minds that the boy (present) with a new scooter.
22. The boss assured the stuff they (tell) about the coming changes. "Toy (tell) of my future plans", he said.
23. Don't worry! The burglars (catch) by the police. – Hm, but they are sure they (not catch).

24. Get your passport ready, they (examine) by the officer. Do toy remember we were warned that our papers (examine) here?
25. The hole nation hoped he (elect) Prime-Minister.
26. Mind, you (punish) if you disobey my orders.
27. I wonder when my project paper (publish).
28. The child (bring up) in a respectable family.
29. They made sure that the child (bring up) by the decent people.
30. Don't leave your outside. It (steal).
31. When he turns up he (tell) the truth.
32. The new spaceship (launch) in Florida in some days.
33. The delegation (meet) at the airport.
34. No one expected that the flight (delay).
35. We felt happy that the car (repair) the next day.

Ex. 8. Put the sentences into the Passive voice.

1. They are pulling down the old theatre.
2. People are spending far more money on food now.
3. The librarian says that they are starting a new system because people were not returning books.
4. They are building a new road here.
5. Mike is doing a lot of work.
6. They will be lengthening the runways at all the main airports.
7. It is now 6 a.m. and at most of the hospitals in the country they are awakening patients with cup of tea.
8. They were towing the damaged ship «Titanic» into harbour when the tow-line broke.
9. She is still typing the letters.
10. They were taking more effective measures at the time.
11. They will be building a new movie theatre in this square next year.
12. They are examining the students in room 206.
13. The government is spending little money on roads.
14. They were throwing stones into the sea.
15. Your can't go in. They are interviewing her for the TV.
16. Our scientists are examining a new spaceship.
17. Our friends are making preparation to meet them.
18. They are preparing the meal now.
19. Tom and Harry were carrying our suitcases.
20. They will be discussing a very important question at the meeting tomorrow.

Ex. 9. Put the verbs in brackets into the Present Simple or Present Progressive Passive.

1. Such mistakes (make) by even the best students.
2. The houses (build) of stone, brick and wood.
3. A new museum now (open).
4. A special rule (make) for students to be taken to the University.
5. The goods (examine) at the moment.
6. Papers (deliver) usually at 8 in the morning, they (look through) at the moment and you'll get yours soon.
7. Dress (make) preferably of cotton in hot countries. This wonderful costume (make) specially for this performance now.
8. - What strange sounds!
- Oh, our piano (tune).

9. - Where is your car?
10.- It (fill) usually on the garage at the moment.
11.Tea (lay) usually on the balcony in fine weather.
12.We are finishing the last preparations for the party: the lights (switch on), the tables (lay). Do toy think we'll be ready on time?
13.I've got two questions to you. First: «What language (speak) all over the world?» Second: «What language (speak) in this room?»
14.The witness (question) by the police-inspector now.
15.The old motorway (use) by many people, but it's not very convent, that's why a new ring-road (build) in the city.
16.Our luggage (examine) at the Custom now. Any luggage going abroad (check) usually here.
17.We (give) a lot of advice by our parents.
18.All the contacts (sign) by the President.
19.You'll have your copy soon, the contract (type).
20.Lots of people (operate on) in this clinic. And now unfortunately my uncle John (operate) on here.

Ex. 10. Put the verbs in brackets into Past Simple or Past Progressive Passive form.

1.The student (ask) to tell the story again.
2.While the professor (speak) no sound was uttered.
3.A modern tune (play) when we came into the hall.
4.Every morning the boys (tell) what they had to do.

5.I sat down for a rest while the repairs (do).

6.At last the problem (solve) to everyone's satisfaction.

7.The life of man (change) by the Industrial Revolution in the 19th century.

8.A week ago the students of our group (choose) for jury service.

9.The game (play) with zest by both teams.

10.Last Friday he (meet) at the railway station.

11.Many towns (destroy) by the earthquake in Japan last year.

12. The helicopter (construct) in Russia.

13.He (throw) out of class cheating.

14.The pop singers arrived at the airport and (welcome) by thousands of fans. Flowers (throw) at them all the way to the exit.

15.The exposition (open) when we drove up to the picture gallery.

16.He couldn't go out as his suit and shirt (clean).

17.The petrol tank (fill) last week.

18.The policeman noticed that the suitcase (carry) by the porter in a most strange way.

19.The naughty boy (teach) a very good lesson by his friends.

20.When I came to the skating-rink he (teach) to skate by his elder brother.

21.His cousin (fine) for exceeding speed limit yesterday.

22.I drove up to the shop just as it (close), but the owner was kind enough to let me in.

23.They (award) the highest prize.

24.She watched television while the dinner (prepare).

25.When I came into the kitchen I smelt something delicious. My favourite cookies (bake) in the oven.

Ex. 11. Put the sentences into the Passive Voice.

1)

1. The secretary has recently brought this letter.
2. Jack has just spilled the milk.
3. My little brother has broken this cup.
4. She has dusted the room carefully.
5. He felt better when he had reached the post office, bought a registered envelope and posted the letter.
6. By the time the director came she had typed the letters.
7. They went home after they had finished the work.

8. He wondered why we had not visited him before.
9. car has been lent to me for the week.
10. They will have passed the exams by the end of June.
11. Somebody had cleaned my shoes and brushed my suit.
12. Previous climbers had cut steps in the ice.
13. We shall have finished this report by 6 o'clock.
14. Somebody had slashed the picture with a knife.
15. The burglars had cut an enormous hole in the steel door.
16. Someone has already told her to report for duty at six.
17. Compare clothes which we have washed with clothes which any other laundry has washed.
18. The author will have written a special edition for children by the end of the year.
19. Have they bought the books?
20. Nobody have noticed the girl.
21. Have you given the children their milk?
22. What have you done about it?
23. They have built the house in record time.
24. By the time he came we had done it all.
25. They have proved the scientific theory to be false.

2)

1. Someone told us a very funny story yesterday.
2. The people gave him a hearty welcome.
3. They have offered my brother a very good job.
4. The house agents showed us very nice flats.
5. The secretary didn't tell me the exact time of my appointment.
6. They have never taught that that rood boy good manners.
7. The teacher hasn't asked Peter any questions at this lesson.
8. People wished the newly married couple a long and happy life.
9. They never tell me the family news.
10. The examiners didn't give us enough time to answer all the questions.
11. A guide will show the tourists most of the sights of London.
12. They waste a lot of time discussing unimportant things.
13. They type the letters in the other office. They will type yours in a minute.
14. They are repairing my piano at the moment.
15. The guests ate all the sandwiches, and drank all the lemonade. They lest nothing.

16. Has someone posted my parcel.
17. Why did no one informed me of the change of the plan?
18. I'm afraid we have sold all our copies but we have ordered more.
19. They haven't stamped the letter.
20. She didn't introduce me to her mother.
21. An earthquake destroyed the town.
22. He didn't tell me the whole truth.

Ex. 12 Put the verbs in brackets into the Past Simple Passive or Present Perfect Passive.

1. The decorations (complete) an hour ago.
2. The preparations for the party just (finish) and the guests are already arriving.
3. The baby (feed) an hour ago.
4. Christopher (feed) yet? - Not yet.
5. He (not see) for a week already.
6. The paper (not ready) by anyone yet.
7. The suit (not wear) for a long time.
8. This fact (not mention) in his last speech.
9. I'm happy as I just (allow) to stay here for an extra day.
10. She (teach) music in her childhood.
11. You ever (teach) how to play chess?
12. I just (advise) to keep to a diet.
13. The sportsmen (give) instructions before the match.
14. The motorist (disqualify) some five months ago.
15. I can't believe my eyes! My book (publish) already!
16. It is really fantastic! I have finished my task in time!
17. Are you not looking outside? The sky is full of clouds!
18. I am (direction) to keep slow on highways.
19. People (get) instruction about proper use of water.
20. My programme was (final) last night by friends.
21. Have you ever (get) proper training to drive a car?
22. Children (feed) during last interval of the show.
23. Half of the team members (board) the bus.
24. All people (reach) the site, we are about to move.
25. Corps (evacuate) the site which was flooded last night.
26. Single windw system of service was (open) by members.

Exercise 9

Q 1. Complete the text with expressions given below.

> had been given had been told   had never been taught
> was given *(twice)*   was offered   was promised
> was shown   wasn't being paid   was sent

I'll never forget my first day at that office. I __(1)__ to arrive at 8.30, but when I got there the whole place seemed to be empty. I didn't know what to do, because I __(2)__ no information about the building or where I was going to work, so I just waited around until some of the secretaries began to turn up. Finally I __(3)__ a dirty little office on the fifth floor, where I __(4)__ a desk in a corner. Nothing happened for an hour; then I __(5)__ some letters to type on a computer by one of the senior secretaries. This wasn't very successful, because I __(6)__ how to use a computer. (in the letter I __(7)__ when I __(8)__ the job, I __(9)__ computer training, but they'd obviously forgotten about this.) By lunchtime things hadn't got any better, and I decided that I __(10)__ enough to put up with the nonsense, so I walked out and didn't go back.

Q 2. A press conference is being held. Put in the correct forms of the verbs. Dramatise the dialogue.

1. Reporter: Can this new drug prolong human life?

    Professor: yes, we believe that human life can be prolonged by the drug.
2. R.: Are you going to do any more tests on the drug?

    P.: Yes, further tests ______ .
3. R. What ______ the drug ______ ?

    P.: It will be called Bio-Meg.
4. R.: Can people use the drug now?

    P.: No, the drug ______ yet.
5. R.: Who will produce the drug?

    P.: It ______ by the Bentrix drug company.
6. R. Do you think they should sell it to anyone who wants it?

    P.: Yes, I think it ______ freely.

7. R.: And what quantity could Bentrix produce?
   P.: We believe the drug ______ in large quantities.

Q 3. *You are telling a friend some news. Use the notes and write each sentence in the Present Perfect, active (has done) or passive (has been done).*

1. (Someone — repair — phone box)
   You know the phone box at the end of the road? It has been repaired.
2. (Trevor — leave — his wife)
   Have you heard about Trevor? ________________.
3. (Someone — steal — Kate's — new car)
   You know about Kate's new car? ____________.
4. (Parkers — buy — video camera)
   You know the Parkers? They _________.
5. (An ambulance — take — Mr. Deacon — hospital)
   Poor old Mr. Deacon! He ____________.
6. (Owner — sell — house)
   You know the house on the corner? It ___________.
7. (Picture — win — the competition)
   You remember that picture Mark painted? _____________.
8. (Company — sack — Caroline)
   I feel sorry for Caroline. ____________.
9. (Something — run over — cat)
   Bad news about the cat next door! _____________!

Q 4. *Complete this conversation with verbs in a suitable tense, active or passive. Learn the dialogue by heart.*

Cindy and Petra are members of a volleyball team.
C. Why wasn't Claire at the training session?
P. Haven't you heard? She has been (1) thrown out for stealing.
C. No! Really?
P. Yes! She ___(2)___ taking money from someone's bag in the changing room.
C Who by?
P. The sports club manager. She ___(3)___ through the changing room when she ___(4)___.
C. Oh, dear… That's terrible!

P. Claire said she __(5)__ to fetch the money by Karen, but when Karen __(6)__ about it, she said she __(7)__ (not) what Claire was talking about.

C. But how stupid of Karen to leave money in the changing room!

P. Yes! She __(8)__ that by the manager too.

C. She __(9)__ (not) it again, anyhow.

P. No, I guess not. What do you think Claire __(10)__ now?

C. I don't know. This is the second club she __(11)__ to leave, isn't it?

P. Yes. It's hard to know what can __(12)__ for someone like Claire.

Q 5. Who by? Group work. Match the two columns. Then make a sentence for each, using the passive. Look at the example first.

Example: I think penicillin was discovered by Alexander Fleming.

1. *Guernica*	Margaret Mitchell
2. Radium	Picasso
3. Penicillin	Agatha Christie
4. *Rashomon*	Thomas Edison
5. Light bulbs	Madonna
6. *Gone with the Wind*	Alexander Fleming
7. Walkman Stereo	Walt Disney
8. Mickey Mouse	MGIMO University
9. *Material Girl*	Sony
10. *War and Peace*	Marie Curie
11. This booklet	Akira Kurosawa
12. *Murder on the Orient Express*	Leo Tolstoy

Q 6. It has to be redecorated!

A) Before Maria and Brian can move into their new apartment, it has to be redecorated. Amy and Bob are doing the work for them.

Change these sentences using the passive.

1. They gave the job to Amy and Bob.
2. They started the work last week.
3. They finished the kitchen on Monday.
4. They were doing the bedroom on Friday.
5. They are painting the living room now.
6. They have painted the walls green.
7. They are going to paint the ceiling pink.

8.   They are going to finish the work next week.

B) *Pair work.*

Look at the decoration of the room you are in now. Talk about what has been done and what needs to be done.

Q 7. Pair work.: Imagine that your apartment was redecorated while you were on vacation.. Unfortunately, your instructions were not followed. Your partner should find out what was done wrong in your apartment. These are the instructions that were left for the painter. You can see what was done right: **blue √,** and what was done wrong: **white** — *pale green* (pale green instead of white)

	DOOR	**WALLS**	**CEILING**
Kitchen	Blue √	White — *pale green*	White — *pink*
Study	Dark green √	Pale green — *white*	Green — *red*
Living room	Tan √	Tan — *brown*	White — *tan*
Hall	Blue — *red*	Pale blue √	Grey — *blue*
Front door	White — *grey*		
Bedroom	Orange — *red*	Orange √	White √
Bathroom	White — *blue*	Blue — *white*	Pale blue √

Example:
A. Was your kitchen painted all right?
B. No, the kitchen ceiling should have been painted white instead of pink, and walls were painted pale green instead of white.
A. And how about the door?
B. The door was painted blue which was fine.

Q 8. Has everything been done? [Pair work.]

<u>Student A.</u> Imagine that you took your car to be serviced at your local garage, and these are the jobs you wanted them to do. Phone the garage and find out from your partner (owner of the garage) which jobs have been done. Use the pattern: *Has anyone checked the oil?*

<u>Student B</u> Imagine that you work at the garage. Your partner is going to phone you to check which jobs have been done to his/her car. The job that have been done are shown with a check (**√**). Use the patterns:

- *Yes, the oil has been checked.*
- *No, the hood has not been polished yet, but I'll make sure it is done before you get here.*

Check oil √   Fix door lock √

Polish hood   Replace broken headlight bulb √
Install new rear tyres   Change spark plugs
Wash windshield √   Clean out trunk √
Adjust carburator √   Fill tank with gas

Q 9. Present Progressive Passive. Imagine you are in a busy hotel at midday. Make sentences to say what is being done, using words from the list below and Present Progressive Passive. *E.g.: Beds are being made.*

Beds   bills   coffee   drinks   food   luggage
money   new guests   reservations   rooms   tables

Bring down   change clean   lay   make   order
pay   prepare serve   take   welcome

Q 10.Present Perfect Passive. Imagine that, rich and famous, you returned to your old homed after 50 years. A lot of things are different. Make sentences, using words from the list below and the Present Perfect Passive. *E.g.: The Cafe Royal has been turned into a casino.*

Cafe Royal   house boats   new car park   new
schools
opera house   old fire station ring road   station streets
town centre   statue of you   Super Cinema your
house

build   modernise   put up in park   rebuild widen
turn into casino (floating restaurant / museum / supermarket / theatre / pedestrian precinct

***.